# A WOMAN OF SPIRIT

# DORIS COLLINS
# A WOMAN OF SPIRIT

The autobiography of a psychic

Foreword by Michael Bentine

**GRANADA**
London Toronto Sydney New York

Granada Publishing Limited
8 Grafton Street, London W1X 3LA

Published by Granada Publishing 1983

*British Library Cataloguing in Publication Data*

Collins, Doris
  A woman of spirit.
  1. Collins, Doris     2. Clairvoyants—Great Britain
  —Biography
  I. Title
  133.8′4′0924     BF1283.C/

ISBN 0-246-11918 7

Printed in Great Britain by
Richard Clay (The Chaucer Press) Ltd,
Bungay Suffolk

# Foreword by Michael Bentine

During the past fifty years I have been involved with research into the paranormal area of human behaviour. It all started for my family when my father, on his early retirement from science and engineering, decided to investigate what was then called the supernatural or the occult.

Naturally over many years we met and tested a large number of professing mediums, and found most of them to be self-deluded, or even downright charlatans. However, a small proportion of them were undeniably genuine and a very few of those were worth their weight in gold.

Doris Collins, a close friend over a number of years, is truly a part of that golden vein; in fact, she is probably the Mother Lode. Having learnt how to judge genuine mediumship, over many years of searching and researching, I can confidently state that Doris is a remarkable healer and an excellent clairvoyant.

Healing largely consists of transferring energy from the healer to the recipient, and Doris has a super-abundance of that vital life-force which marks the genuine practitioner of the healing art.

I have also seen her produce some extraordinarily effective predictive evidence, in the form of personal messages to people in need of help. To take an outstanding example of these prophetic messages, let me cite the case of a close friend of mine from the United States, who is a highly successful producer of prime-time television programmes. His profession has given him a shrewd and critical attitude to any claims of 'supernatural' phenomena.

Yet, because of the intensely personal and wholly accurate predictive content of certain messages given to him in my home by Doris Collins, he now considers that the life of his wife was saved largely by paranormal means.

Doris told him that their vacation in Britain, which they had planned for months, would end abruptly and then told me privately that she was very concerned, because she had picked up clairvoyantly a *blinding head-pain*.

When, a few days later, my friend's wife was stricken with what was believed to be an aneurism (a 'ballooned' artery) in the head, Doris was able to reassure them both that an operation would be performed in Britain, which would solve their grave problems.

With Doris and myself giving absent healing, a major neurosurgical operation was performed on his wife by skilled surgeons at the London Hospital, and a long-standing *benign* tumour was removed.

Throughout the whole worrying proceedings, both my friends were wonderfully sustained, especially by the healing given to them by Doris, and just as she had predicted, one month later, my wife and I joined our now speedily recuperating friends in Los Angeles. From the time Doris gave my friends those startling messages to our reunion in America, approximately six weeks had passed.

When she is on the platform giving evidential messages through her startling clairvoyance or demonstrating healing to an extraordinary degree of effectiveness, Doris Collins is a superb show-woman, capable of entrancing even the toughest and most critical of audiences, and she does so all over the world.

She truly is a 'woman of spirit' and her book conveys the elusive quality of uniqueness that is a major part of her remarkable personality.

Through these pages you will enjoy meeting this extra-ordinary woman who, while being down-to-earth, is still very much a 'lady with the lamp' of hope, who brings help to the grief-stricken and healing to the sick.

Long may we all enjoy her strength of spirit and enviable faith.

# Acknowledgements

I wish to acknowledge the help and encouragement given to me by Jeffrey Simmons, my husband Philip McCaffrey, Michael and Clementina Bentine, Fanny and Johnny Craddock, Jeraldine Saunders, all my family, and Ray Branch, who suggested the title of the book.

# Chapter One

oⒸooⒸooⒸo

'Doris is different.'

I can still hear my mother's words. I must have been about sixteen at the time; in any case it was roughly three years after my sister Emmie's death. I had been visiting my friends Adeline and Marcia Clasper and I was walking home, deep in thought.

The road is now part of a main motorway leading to Southend, but at the time it was a fairly lonely road with high banks either side, leading from one part of South Woodford to another. The journey would normally have taken me about half an hour and I would have been surprised to have met anyone I knew, or anyone at all for that matter.

It was late afternoon and the day was closing in, but it would still remain light for some time. I was in a somewhat dreamy mood. I saw and heard nobody until suddenly I was startled by a tap on the shoulder.

I was not by nature timid, and it was certainly not my nature to run away from anything, but I was all at once very afraid.

Summoning up my courage, I turned round, and there in a blaze of light were the chiselled features and the dark swept-back hair of my dead sister. I could not have been mistaken and I was not dreaming. I stood rooted to the spot. I had had strange experiences before but this was the first such experience involving a member of my immediate family.

'Don't be afraid, Doris,' I was addressed by name, 'it's only me. It's Emmie.'

1

I could not speak. Emmie and I had never been very close – she was so much older – and her death from tuberculosis had not really affected me. But now, as I looked at her, I had the strong feeling that she wanted to be close to me, perhaps to protect me.

It was only her face I saw. There was no body, although I did not think that odd at the time, at least no odder than that I saw her at all. Just her face in a blazing light. Subsequently, when other people have appeared to me in this way, I have sometimes seen their whole bodies, sometimes just their faces. Sometimes I do not physically see them at all but I get their personality and can even describe what they are wearing, although the image is in my head rather than in my eyes. Seeing is not just done with the eyes.

I had a sense that Emmie was trying to reassure me, to comfort me in some way, but at heart I was terrified, much as I tried to keep my emotions to myself. Before I knew what I was doing, I had taken to my heels and I ran all the way home – two miles or more uphill! I vividly recall banging on the front door and blurting out the story to my parents, not caring whether they believed me or not.

My father was a no-nonsense man and told me I was hallucinating. He sent for Dr Pacey. The doctor surprised him by taking me seriously; at any event, he did not dismiss my story as rubbish.

'Do you believe that you saw Emmie?' he asked me.

'Oh, yes,' I replied, 'she *spoke* to me.'

The doctor nodded. 'When you've seen death as often as I have,' he said, 'it makes you think: is it the end or the beginning?' He gave it as his opinion that there was nothing wrong with me. My father forbade me ever to mention the subject again.

It was my mother however who had the last word. She never doubted me, or if she did she never let me know. 'I don't understand it,' she would sometimes say, 'but if you say so, Doris, I know you're speaking the truth.' On this occasion she took my side against my father. 'Doris is different,' she said. 'Doris is different because I had her so late in life.' My mother was in fact aged forty-eight when I was born.

Whereas my father – eight years her junior – might say, 'We don't want such things discussed,' my mother had a much more open mind. She was probably psychic, although she would not have known what the word meant. She just had her 'feelings' about people. 'I think we'll have a big tea today,' she might say. 'So-and-so is coming.' And although So-and-so had not been invited, So-and-so would usually arrive. She was also very superstitious and would never wear green – which curiously is a colour I often wear. She had one particular superstition, if that is the right word, arising from a story she once told me called 'The Mistletoe Bough' in which a person playing hide-and-seek in a big house disappeared and was found many years later in a trunk. It was not a frightening story the way my mother told it but it had a peculiar significance for her because she claimed to have heard the musical piece of the same title played whenever there was a death in the family.

I was quite a tomboy as a child and often did daring things such as climbing trees that only boys would normally climb, and one day I decided to tempt fate by playing 'The Mistletoe Bough' on the piano. I didn't believe my mother's story anyway, but I made sure that no one was around to hear my performance. Two days later an uncle died.

This put the fear of God into me, not surprisingly; at the age of ten I could not have thought it possible that there could have been any connection between my playing the piano and a family bereavement, but I had not listened to my mother and look what had happened!

3

'It's strange,' my mother said, indicating how seriously she held her belief, 'we haven't heard "The Mistletoe Bough" played. Have you, Doris?'

'No, no,' I was quick to reply.

It was not long afterwards that I tempted fate again, and this time the consequence was immediate. I was still at the piano when there was a crash. I ran into the kitchen to find that an ironing-board that had stood against the wall had collapsed onto the floor, breaking the back of a new-born kitten in its path. I was heartbroken, for I love animals, and this time I confessed to my mother. She was not as angry as I had expected. 'Doris,' was all she said, 'I forbid you ever to play it again.'

It was my mother who taught me to be tolerant and strong. One of my first memories is of her singing to me the words of 'Rock of Ages', the text of which, embroidered in gold and blue, hung on the wall above my cot. 'Rock of ages, cleft for me' – and I think of it even now when I am in trouble, solid and dependable – 'Let me hide myself in thee' – and I remember imagining as a child that I was hiding under the big rock, secure in the knowledge that nobody could find me or hurt me there. It was always my ambition to be strong as the rock.

Perhaps I was 'different', as my mother said, and perhaps it had something to do with my mother's age. I think probably it had more to do with the very extraordinary family into which I was born. Both my parents had been married previously, and both curiously had three boys and a girl from their first marriage. I was thus by far the youngest of nine children, the eldest of whom were old enough to have been my parents!

Brothers George, Fred and John and sister Emmie were the children of my father, George Campbell Cooper, by his first marriage. Will, John (there were two in the family), Stuart and Lilian were my mother's children by her mar-

riage to John Maxwell. She had been born Frances Elizabeth Emerson, and her family were mostly publicans. My
father, like his father before him, was head cooper at
Charrington's Brewery – yes, cooper by trade and Cooper
by name! Curiously, his family had theatrical connections,
which perhaps explains why in later life I found it easy to
speak in public and to demonstrate my healing on the stage
of a meeting hall. Had not my paternal grandmother herself
sung on the stage in her beautiful contralto voice? And had
not another relation, so I was told, appeared regularly as
the cat in pantomime? No one ever let me forget that the
great Gordon Harker was Father's second cousin, and I
knew of course that my father's great friend was no less a
celebrity than Laurie Lupino himself.

Those were names to conjure with at that time, but of
course they meant very little to baby Doris, whose entire
world consisted of her parents, both of whom incidentally
weighed over eighteen stone – my father was six foot four
into the bargain. Despite the large brood into which I was
introduced, I saw very little of the other children. Even the
youngest were some years older than I, whereas the eldest
did not even live at home all the time. I was the only child of
my parents' second marriage, and I was a typical 'only
child'. My parents were very much in love, I believe, and
they lived for each other. I was driven within myself and I
led what most children would have regarded as a lonely
existence.

If I was 'different', as my mother said, it probably had
something to do with that, but I certainly did not think of
myself as lonely. I had a marvellous childhood, and one
thing I never lacked was love – certainly not from my
parents. We always had a dog and cats, which I adored,
and as I grew older I was able to indulge my hobby of
reading. Books appealed to me far more than dolls, and I
grabbed anything I could get my hands on to read.

5

As a very young child, largely I suppose because everyone else was very much older and bigger, I created a world of my own, which possibly explains why I enjoyed books so much. My own world was a world of fantasy which I could not have discussed with my brothers and sisters; they would not have understood it. But my world was crowded with people who were as real to me as they were unreal to my elders.

It was this, strangely, that kept me out of mischief, I think, for how could I misbehave when there was always somebody to observe my every action? I believe I was frightened of being naughty!

If I was different, I did not know it, and indeed it was not until I was five or six that something happened that could indicate that I had perhaps an ability that was either unique to me or at least was not possessed by everybody. I stayed for a short time with an aunt in Manor Park; she was actually the wife of my father's cousin. I used to play in the garden there with a little girl called Connie, a pretty little girl with corkscrew curls. One day I asked my aunt why Connie never came into the house. Looking back, I can see how I must have startled her, for she had had a daughter named Connie who had died some years previously. She questioned me, and I found myself telling her things about the girl that convinced her that I was describing her own daughter, things (so I was told subsequently) that I could not possibly have learnt from my family.

'Connie's dead, darling,' my aunt said. I can picture her anxiety and bewilderment.

'She isn't,' I insisted. 'She talks to me. She's real.'

Readers must form their own conclusions about what I say. I shall not write anything that I am not prepared to justify myself or that I cannot verify. Where I myself have an explanation for something, I will state it for what it is worth, but of course it may not be the right explanation or the only one. I only ask the reader to accept that I am writing what I believe to be the truth, and readers must form their own judgements in the light of their own experience. What I have to say here is that at the tender age of five or six I actually played with a little girl who had died, although at the time I was convinced that she was alive until I was given incontrovertible proof to the contrary. Then, young as I was, I realized for the first time that I was able to contact people who were physically dead.

This is a theme to which I shall return later in the book. I had obviously been born with, or somehow acquired, an unusual gift, which started functioning when I was quite small. I do not suppose that I fully realized this at the time. If I did, the realization did not particularly affect me. I simply took it as a matter of course.

I remember when I was about eight coming home from my Sunday School class. I put all the chairs in a row and imagined that there was a different child on every seat. I then said a prayer, gave a short talk about the Bible and asked the children to join me in a hymn. The show-woman in me had obviously taken control. My mother took it all in her stride. She knocked on the door and called out, 'Time to send all the class home, Doris, lunch is ready.' A couple of my young brothers thought me crazy, and said so.

'That's enough of that,' my mother told them. 'It's just growing up.'

My ever-practical mother always had the right answer. I was of course growing up, but I was still very much in my make-believe world. I always knew the difference however between reality and fantasy. When I imagined the children sitting in their chairs at my prayer meeting, I knew that they were 'pretend' children, that they were not real, although I could have described each one minutely. When I played with Connie in the garden, or later when I met Emmie on my way home, I knew this was reality; this was no pretence.

7

I think I was twelve when I perhaps saved my sister Lily's life in unusual circumstances. My parents almost invariably went out on Saturday night for an evening meal, and on this particular occasion they left me with Lily. I had already gone reluctantly upstairs to bed, but I could hear Lily playing the piano in the parlour downstairs. Something suddenly told me that I had to get her out of the room. It was a voice somewhere in my head. I believe I had occasionally heard voices before, but never with such urgency, and I knew I had to obey, but I was too lazy to get out of bed. I resorted therefore to the childish ploy of calling down to her that I was thirsty and demanding a glass of water.

'You can't have one,' she called back. 'Go to sleep.'

How she expected me to sleep when she was banging away at the piano I could not think, so changing tactics, 'Lily,' I cried, 'I've got a very bad earache. You must put some oil in my ear.'

This little lie worked, for Lily went into the kitchen to fetch the olive oil. Suddenly there was an almighty crash, and this time I did get out of bed. In fact I leapt out and was halfway down the stairs as Lily was starting to run up.

Part of the parlour ceiling had collapsed, and an enormous slab had landed right on the piano stool.

I could not tell my father later that I had been warned by a voice. He would not have believed me. But the experience taught me a lesson I have never ignored from that day on: in future I must obey any message I received in this way.

My father's attitude when confronted by something beyond his experience was to forget it, to put it behind him. When later I saw Emmie in circumstances I have already described, he forbade me to refer to the matter again. 'We don't want such things discussed,' were his final words on the subject.

Much as I respected him however I simply could not let

the matter of Emmie drop. It had made too serious an impression on me, and by then I was in any case already a young adult. I had to share my experience with someone else.

Marcia Clasper was the girl who sat next to me at school, and it was she to whom I confided the extraordinary story of my meeting Emmie. Somewhat to my surprise, she accepted what I told her. She believed me. She had, she said, heard similar stories from her mother, who was a psychic.

It was the first time I had heard the word. 'What's a psychic?' I asked.

Marcia was unable to explain, but she suggested that I should meet her mother. I knew instinctively that such a meeting would not have the approval of my parents, certainly not of my father, and I hesitated; but the urge was too strong, and after much soul-searching I agreed to go with Marcia to her mother.

What was I letting myself in for? I had never met a psychic and I had visions of some two-headed monster or perhaps one of the witches from *Macbeth*; but on the other hand, since Mrs Clasper was the mother of Adeline and Marcia, she could not be all that bad. She turned out in fact to be a perfectly ordinary-looking woman, middle-aged I presumed, thinnish, with dark hair and a sallow complexion – in every way unremarkable. She was a retiring lady, and by no means the dynamic personality I had imagined.

It was not of course her appearance that impressed me, but what she told me. She told me that she was regarded as a medium and that she had psychic powers, and she explained what that meant, as she understood it. I must not be afraid, she told me; many people were psychic, some without knowing it, but those who were able to recognize the quality in themselves could develop it if they wished. Being psychic was something good, particularly if one put it to the right use and did not abuse it.

It was Mrs Clasper who first revealed to me that I had the

psychic gift – for that is how she regarded it – and perhaps she was only telling me what I had begun to suspect for myself. The gift was more strongly developed in me, she said, than in most people. It was something with which I had obviously been born. I must realize it and use it wisely.

Perhaps subconsciously I had been afraid of it, but immediately I was afraid no more, especially when Mrs Clasper told me: 'You'll work with this gift, I can see. In fact you have the great power of healing. You'll go all over the world using this power.'

I left my meeting with her with my spirit uplifted. I felt I had a purpose in life, that I would be able to help people. Mrs Clasper had shown me the way ahead. Indeed she set me on the path that I have trodden ever since.

I was still only a girl however and I did not feel able to discuss such matters with my parents, but the day soon came when I was compelled to confront my father with my 'gift'. I had regularly passed the local spiritualist church without ever attending one of its services. I am a religious person in the ordinary sense of the word and I had been brought up to go every Sunday to the neighbourhood church where my parents worshipped. One Sunday I excused myself from accompanying them – I no longer remember what excuse I made – and went instead to the spiritualist service. It was of course different from what I had been used to, but I could never have anticipated how dramatic my first visit there would turn out.

At a point during the ceremony, a woman who had been sitting on the platform where the proceedings were largely conducted came down into the congregation and made straight for me. 'I've got your sister Emmie here,' she said, in front of an entire audience. 'She tells me she frightened you, but you must give your father a message from her.'

'Oh, I can't do that,' I blurted out. 'He doesn't know I'm here.'

'She says,' the woman continued, '"Will you tell Dad I'm sorry, and will he forgive me for what I did? I know now he was right."'

Just what this meant I could not fathom, and I wondered whether it would make sense to my father – if I dared pass it on, that is, for had I not been forbidden ever again to mention Emmie? My father, as I have said, was no mean figure of a man, and with his spectacles hanging over his nose in very forbidding fashion, he could be quite a formidable proposition in the eyes of a teenage girl who was being asked to defy him.

It took me several weeks in fact to pluck up courage and pass on the message. I was always confident of my father's love, but I thought he would be very angry. However, I just *had* to give him the message in case it was important, and I must suffer the consequences. 'Dad,' I said, 'I've got a message from Emmie' – and before he could say anything, I passed it on to him word for word as I had remembered it from the spiritualist meeting and as I had rehearsed it every day since.

His reaction was totally unexpected. In fact there was no reaction at first, just a long silence. I saw Mother look at him. Then finally he asked me, 'Where did you get that message?'

There was nothing I could do except tell him the truth. 'Where is this place?' he enquired. 'Next Sunday we'll all go.'

I could hardly believe my ears. That evening my mother told me that Emmie had made what my father regarded as a bad marriage. She had married against his wishes and he had forbidden her the house. So the message had a very real meaning for him.

The following Sunday, Mother, Father and I went together to the spiritualist church. We took up the entire back row, for I have never exactly been a sylph-like figure

11

myself! I do not think that my father had any notion of becoming a regular congregant. This was more likely his sign of support for me. He did not have to tell me in words: I knew that he believed in me.

From that day on I began deliberately to cultivate my gifts.

# Chapter Two

oⒸooⒸooⒸo

I had been known in school as Coop. 'Go to Coop,' children who had problems were often told, 'she'll help you.' I had a reputation for sorting out their little difficulties; fortunately nobody ever came to me with any serious ones, for I had led a comparatively sheltered childhood and was not very sophisticated or aware of the ways of the world.

I must in fact have been very naive when I left school at the age of fifteen and, at my father's insistence but much against my own wishes, studied shorthand, typing and book-keeping at commercial school in Walthamstow. I hated every minute of it. I did not want to spend my life shut up in an office, and if I had any ambition it was to be a nurse.

Naive I may have been, but I was never unadventurous, and on my own initiative I got a job as a swimming instructor at the Kingfisher swimming pool, newly opened in Woodford. I had been champion swimmer of my school, as well as being captain of sports, and I far preferred an atmosphere in which I could work in the open and among a wide variety of people. I liked people – and have continued to do so all my life.

My father was furious. 'Why can't you knuckle down to commercial work?' he demanded. 'I don't call this any sort of employment. It's a shilly-shally job.'

I knew he would not allow me to remain at the swimming pool, so in anticipation of his redirecting me along commercial paths, I followed another inclination and applied for a job as a nurse: not just an ordinary nurse – that was not

13

good enough for young Doris – but a mental nurse. Had I not always been drawn to people with problems? Unknown again to my parents, I went to see the matron of Claybury Mental Hospital in Woodford. I told her I was eighteen, which was only a slight exaggeration, and I looked older than my years in any case. In fact it was because I looked strong, and could therefore help with difficult cases, that she said I could start as a probationer.

I found that I had indeed jumped in at the deep end, for after the minimum of training I was on duty in one of the worst wards in the hospital, having to wash a completely bedridden patient whose body was covered with sores. When another nurse told me about her condition, it meant nothing to me. I had never heard of venereal disease. Sex was a subject that was never discussed at home. I shall never forget the look in the patient's eyes as I struggled to hide my distaste and to wash her. It was as though her soul was speaking to me. I was horrified, and the whole thing was a nightmare, but in some way I realized that I was helping a human being and that helping people was one of my functions in life. So strong was this feeling that long after I had left this job – after my second marriage in fact – I returned to the hospital for a year as a night nurse, getting up and going to bed at strange hours because I felt I had left a job unfinished.

If my father had been furious when I took the job of swimming instructor, he was doubly so when I explained to him that I wanted to help people who were sick in their minds. 'If you're going to be a nurse, be a *nurse*,' he shouted. I know now that he was only motivated in his advice to me by his love for me, but at the time he seemed very dictatorial. I admit that I was not entirely happy at the hospital, and it was Father who did something about it.

He contacted a distant relative who worked as a government inspector for the Crown Agents for the Colonies. One of his functions was to control the printing of banknotes and stamps, and he had an office at the firm of De La Rue, who carried out work of this nature for many countries throughout the world. My father thought that, although I did not want to be shut away in an office, the variety of work at the Crown Agents might appeal to me. In this he was correct.

The first thing the inspector told me when I went for an interview was that the work was very responsible, and this was exactly what I wanted. I was accepted for the job and I was trained to examine banknotes and stamps for errors. I loved it. If there was the slightest error on a sheet of stamps and a dealer got hold of it, he could make a fortune out of it. A slight discoloration, for example, or an absence of perforation could increase the value of the sheet enormously. Even a small tear under the Sovereign's eye could turn a penny stamp into an object of value.

Sometimes one could inspect half a dozen batches of stamps or notes without detecting an imperfection; sometimes one might find something wrong with perhaps one note in five hundred. The margin of error was small, but the consequences big. Hence the responsibility of the work.

I am amazed at how many errors one finds in a newspaper nowadays, but when I was young they were much rarer. I remember a publisher's reader once telling me that he could just look at a page and spot a mistake; his hawk eye was drawn to it like a moth to a flame. In my case I had a feeling when something was wrong. I cannot explain it exactly except to say that it was like a psychic sensing. I would be inspecting a batch of sheets in the manner I had been taught when suddenly I would go back on a sheet I had passed and find the error I had missed the first time. I may be wrong but I think it was something I had sensed rather than something I had actually seen in my mind's eye.

I was not particularly conscious of any psychic occurrences at that time, and I did not have any very startling

15

experiences of the sort I had encountered as a young child. Perhaps it was that I was too busy making a life for myself, or perhaps I was no longer so solitary. I now had boyfriends and an interesting job.

My life changed when I met Jack. I never knew why everybody called him Jack, because his real name was Ernest Bewley Lawless. My big brother John Maxwell had a hotel in Barking, and on one of my visits there I met John's friend Jack, who was a steward aboard SS *Orion*, which used to make the voyage to Australia and back. He was the first man I had met socially, apart from family, who was not my own age; he was sixteen years my senior. I had never met anyone with such charming manners, or, as it seemed to me at the time, so sophisticated – certainly not anyone who took an interest in me.

In his letters – for he started to write to me – he described every detail of his voyages, the places he went to, the people he met. I think I fell in love with his letters. When he came home on leave, this meant two glamorous weeks for me. For the first time in my life I sat in a box at the opera. We had a box too for Sonja Henie's ice show from which I looked down on the theatre circle where some colleagues from work were sitting; they could hardly believe their eyes when they saw me with such a dashing companion.

Jack had never been married but he proposed to me after only two voyages to Australia and back. It was then that I really discovered how tough my father could be. 'You're far too old for my daughter,' he told Jack. 'When you want to put your feet up, she'll be wanting to kick her heels up dancing. I know my Doris. She likes life.'

That was the least of it. A carefree bachelor, Jack had been used to spending every penny he earned. 'What are your prospects?' Father enquired. 'I don't approve of my daughter marrying anyone who goes away to sea.'

I asked if I could get engaged. 'Not with my permission,' was the reply.

My mother, who was by nature a peacemaker, never made judgements. She thought I was foolish but she would not take sides. She only warned me that if I did become engaged, I should not wear the ring in front of Father. But I was my father's daughter, as stubborn as he, and next time I went home I flaunted my engagement ring for all to see. My father pretended not to notice. This infuriated me, so I told him I was engaged to Jack.

'As far as I'm concerned,' he said, 'you're not engaged, and I don't want to discuss it further.' He did not speak to me, except through Mother, for the next six months!

Jack did not make matters any better by giving up the sea. He took a job as a book-keeper. Father was speaking to me again by then. 'This is the worst day's work you've ever done,' he told me. 'What do you think you're going to live on, you who've never had to know the value of money?'

Looking back, my father was probably right, and I remembered Emmie appearing to me and the message she had wanted me to pass on to him. I think that had he been less adamant, his headstrong daughters might have been more conciliatory, but in any case his attitude arose entirely from his concern and love for his children – I know that now.

I insisted on marrying and I gave up my job with the Crown Agents. Six days before I was twenty-one, and incidentally seven months before war broke out, I married Jack at a register office in Ilford. I had always wanted a church wedding, but I thought in the circumstances it was better to get the matter behind me as quickly as possible. I had found a flat in Ilford and I had been given a lump sum when I left my job; with Jack's salary we would not starve.

Perhaps realizing that we needed money more than anything, Father gave me a substantial cheque as a wedding present. Jack wanted to return it. 'We don't need his money,' he said.

'I can give what I like to my daughter,' was Father's response. 'She may be marrying you, but she's still my daughter. Experience tells me that when she marries you, she'll need every penny.' That was that, and I kept the money.

In hindsight I can see that my father probably gave me the right advice, the sort of advice that a loving parent should have given and that a sensible daughter should perhaps have heeded, but for a long time our marriage was quite happy and my family came to accept the situation. We visited my parents every Sunday for lunch, which I believe was one small way in which my parents thought they were helping us financially! My husband's father and a brother were dead, and he supported his mother and two sisters, so any little help was welcome.

My son Brian was born in July 1940 – a real wartime baby of course. My father wanted me to have my baby at home – at his home in fact – since in those days it was far less usual than it has since become to go to hospital. Something told me however that I should have my child in the local maternity hospital. It was not a voice, it was nothing in particular, just a feeling. The pregnancy had been quite normal and I had no reason to expect any complications, but my conviction was so strong that I actually quarrelled with my father over the matter.

Thank God I obeyed my instinct, or whatever it was that guided me. I woke up one Monday morning and knew at once that I would have to go to hospital that day, although the doctor had thought that the baby would not arrive that week. I telephoned my father to say that the baby was starting, and I asked him in turn to telephone first my husband and then the ambulance to take me to Plaistow Maternity Hospital. I do not know why I contacted Father rather than Jack; perhaps I thought Father more reliable.

I remember lying in bed in hospital when suddenly I experienced a pain the like of which I had never known. My yell must have sounded like a bomb dropping. At all events it attracted the immediate entrance of a big Irish nurse.

'Mrs Lawless,' she said incredulously – although I suspect this was not the first yell she had heard – 'did I hear you utter a sound?'

'Yes, nurse,' I replied meekly, 'the pain was bad.'

'Thousands of mothers have babies every day,' she admonished me as if I were a naughty child. 'You're no different. Don't let me hear you utter another cry.'

She knew of course that it is bad to yell in such circumstances because, in doing so, one draws in one's breath, and her sensible advice or instruction was obviously given with this fact in mind rather than to preserve the peace and tranquillity of her domain. Although I did not realize this at the time, her manner of speaking had the desired effect on me. I determined not in any circumstances to utter a sound.

It was then that I discovered for myself a technique for riding pain. This is a technique I have since taught, which is often taught nowadays to expectant mothers, but which at the time was not so well known. Methods of relaxation are today explained in almost all ante-natal clinics, but they were either unknown forty years ago or people were too busy fighting a war to bother with them.

I thought as I lay there that when the pain came again I would ride on top of it, as I might on top of a huge wave in the ocean. As the pain increased, so I rose higher in the air; as it decreased, I went with it into its trough. If we had lived in Australia or Hawaii, perhaps Brian would have become a surfrider, for he was certainly born on the crest of the waves.

19

It was a difficult, even dangerous, birth and it was just as well for me that I had insisted on being in hospital. I had already had two blood transfusions when they sent for Jack. His blood group was the same as mine and almost the first thing they did when he arrived in the middle of the night was to take two pints from him and give me another two transfusions.

Little Brian Campbell Lawless came into this world an apparently normal baby, and no one was particularly worried when he became very jaundiced two or three days later. The doctors and nurses did all that was necessary and I had a healthy son. I was not to know that he would later develop a rare complaint, as I shall explain.

My father died just over two years later. He was only sixty-three. It was all very sudden. He had been complaining of chest pains and one day walked into the London Hospital in the Mile End Road, feeling sick. They took him in and put him in a wheelchair. Four days later he had a heart attack from which he did not recover.

God had spared him long enough to know my son, and I can only wish that he had lived long enough to know my daughter too, but I did not adopt Margaret until three years after his death. I had given birth to a son who had lived only a few hours the year before. I was told that it was risky to have another child, particularly after the difficult time I had had with Brian and what had happened with baby John. There was so much love in me, and I was so upset about John, that I discussed with Jack the possibility of adopting another child, perhaps a little girl. It was agreed that I should make enquiries.

In fact it took some time before we were approved as suitable parents, even during the war. Eventually I received a letter from the home I had contacted. They were shortly expecting the arrival of a mother-to-be who wanted her baby to be adopted, and would I consent to take the child? I

20

had to agree unconditionally to take the baby, whatever its sex, provided that it was normal. I did not think twice before replying, although I hoped for a girl because I already had a boy. You can imagine my joy when my lovely daughter Margaret Ann arrived, and I am delighted to add that she – no less than Brian – has continued to be a joy to me all my life.

She came to me when she was sixteen days old, and her arrival in a way heralded the end of the war, just as Brian's had marked its beginning.

My mother meantime had gone to live in Leigh-on-Sea in Essex. She had gone to pieces at first after the death of Father, with whom she had been so very much in love and around whom she had made her existence. Death can be a shattering experience in such circumstances for the surviving partner, as I know only too well from the thousands of people who have come to me for help and advice – or, as I prefer to think of it, mental healing – over the years. I know that death is not final and that the dead are often with us, and I shall have something to say on that subject later; but even such knowledge cannot do much more than comfort at the moment of bereavement.

I am not sure that my mother was very enthusiastic about my adopting Margaret, but they came to adore each other, and I took the children as often as I could to the seaside to visit her. From time to time, as often as I could persuade her, she came to stay with us, and I know that Margaret was a great inducement; there was a strong rapport between them.

It was just before Christmas in 1949. Margaret was not yet five and Brian was already a strapping nine-year-old. I had a feeling one morning that Mother was sick. There was no reply when I telephoned, so I rang her neighbour who confirmed that she was indeed ill, although there was nothing serious. 'Don't let my Doris know,' Mother had told the neighbour, 'because she'll be down here with an ambulance.'

I then phoned her doctor who told me that she had bronchitis and was not improving very rapidly. I asked whether she could travel, and he said that the benefit to her of being with her family would probably outweigh the slight risk involved in moving her. My mother was seventy-eight.

I went to fetch her. 'Oh, I knew you'd come,' she said. I think she was glad to return with me.

I had spoken to my own doctor and arranged to put a bed for Mother in a downstairs room. It was the 23rd of December and I was busily putting up the Christmas tree, dressing a doll for Margaret and doing all the things that a housewife and mother has to do at that time of year. I had to go out to do some last-minute shopping, so I put an easy chair by the side of her bed in case she wanted to get up for a few moments while I was out.

I moved the chair when I came back. 'Oh, Doris,' my mother said, 'you are a naughty girl. You moved the chair.'

'You don't need it now that I'm back,' I said, somewhat surprised by the tone of her voice.

'My brother Bill was sitting there with me,' she explained. 'Now you've moved the chair, he's gone.'

I stopped to think. Her brother Bill was the one member of her family she never spoke about, because it was he who had accidentally struck a blow that killed her first husband. I had been told the story by relations – not by her – and I had been led to believe that there had been no animosity between Mother and her brother; she just chose never to discuss the matter, understandably. Bill, she now said, had been sitting with her all afternoon.

People do hallucinate, particularly under the influence of drugs, but I believed that my mother was speaking the truth when she told me she had seen her brother Bill. I had had stranger experiences myself, and I was perhaps better

22

qualified than most people to distinguish between fact and fantasy in this sort of instance. Perhaps indeed I had inherited my gift from my mother, who undoubtedly had psychic powers.

Whatever the truth, I felt somehow that the appearance of Bill had some significance for Mother. Why do you think he came?' I asked.

Her reply startled me. 'I'm going to die,' she said. I had had no thought that my mother might be nearing death, despite her years. 'Don't be silly,' I said, 'you're going to get better.'

When the doctor came the following day she went straight to the telephone, after examining Mother, and rang the hospital. 'I'm getting your mother into hospital,' she told me, as if the decision had nothing to do with me.

'Whatever for?' I asked.

'It's her request,' was the reply.

'I don't believe it,' I said, perhaps somewhat rudely, but what possible reason could my mother have for wanting to move on Christmas Eve, of all times? The doctor suggested that I speak to Mother myself, and I confess that I was rather cross with her. 'Oh, Doris,' she said, 'don't you understand? It's Christmas. You've got a lot to do without my being in your way. In any case, it's better for me.'

I felt that I had to respect her wishes, and I rode with her in the ambulance to King George's Hospital in Ilford. On the way, she gave me her engagement ring. 'I'm going to die, Doris, you know,' she said. 'I have no regrets. I've had a good life. I want you to have my engagement ring now, and I want you to promise me that you'll take off my wedding ring too, but not until I die.'

It was late at night when the hospital phoned. 'Your mother's taken a turn for the worse,' I was told. 'Can you come at once?'

I knew then that Mother was already dead, and I said so.

23

'Actually yes,' the caller admitted, 'but we didn't like to break it to you like that. Will you come then in the morning to identify the body? It's something that has to be done.'

When I arrived, I was met by the sister. She was holding Mother's wedding ring. 'Your mother made me take it off and told me to give it to you when you came,' she said.

My darling mother had made her own arrangements, and she had not wanted to die in my house at Christmas with my little children at home.

# Chapter Three

oᗤooᗤooᗤo

I am a very ordinary person who happens to have a gift or gifts that most ordinary people do not possess, or if they do possess them, do not develop. I say gift or gifts because I distinguish to some extent between Doris Collins the psychic and Doris Collins the healer. There is of course a connection between my work as a psychic and as a spiritual healer, but one does not need to be psychic to heal.

I began seriously to take an interest in healing soon after my marriage, when I was twenty-two, but for about five years before that I had been interesting myself in spiritual-ism and making friends among spiritualists. I am by nature a very logical person, and I will always find a logical answer to a problem whenever possible, so it is strange perhaps that my gift is essentially illogical, by which I mean that it often manifests itself in ways that cannot always be ex-plained by logic as we understand it.

Following my introduction to the Woodford Spiritualist Church by Mrs Clasper, when I received the message for my father from Emmie, I used to visit the church occa-sionally on Sundays. On one such visit I was approached by a stranger whose name was Bull who said that he had been observing me and that I had definite psychic ability. He asked if I was interested in developing my talent. If so, would I join his development circle which met every Tuesday evening at his home in Wanstead?

I asked what a development circle was, and he said that it was a group of friends, men and women, who got together because of their common interest in spiritualism.

I was only seventeen and was not quite sure what I was

letting myself in for, but my curiosity overcame my anxiety and I found myself ringing the bell of Mr Bull's tall house the following week. He answered the door himself. 'Come in,' he said, 'and meet the friends.'

I went into a drawing-room in the centre of which a dozen or so chairs had been placed in a circle. We chatted as if at a cocktail party where no drinks were served, and when everybody had assembled, we were asked to take our seats. I was placed in a chair directly opposite the one occupied by our host. The main light was turned off and a small table lamp with a red bulb was switched on in its place. I was somewhat apprehensive, but my neighbour explained that they got better results in the semi-darkness.

Mr Bull said a short prayer, asking for God's guidance and protection. Somehow the light was dimmed even more until very little could be seen. We were told to meditate.

I have since learnt the art of meditation, and have taught it. It can be most helpful. At the time, however, it was something I had never seriously tried. I know now that an hour's meditation can pass seemingly in five minutes, but at that time five minutes seemed to drag for me into an hour. I was rather detached, I think, wondering what all the others were meditating about, who they were, and whether I would be all right. All of a sudden there was a terrific bang, and it seemed to come from right behind my chair.

I was too scared to turn round and look, and I gripped the side of the chair. I do not know how long it was before the light was turned up, but eventually Mr Bull got up and turned on the main light after warning us to shield our eyes until they became accustomed again to the brightness. I still did not look behind me, and I wondered if any of the others had heard anything; if they had, they made no sign of having done so.

Then in turn we were asked to say what we had been meditating about. As my turn approached I listened to what others were saying about the various thoughts that had passed through their minds, and nobody mentioned having heard any sort of noise. Surely I was not the only one to have heard the bang, or was it that I was the only one who had not been meditating properly?

When it came to me, I plucked up courage. I said that I had tried to have 'nice thoughts' but that I had not really thought much about anything. I had however been disturbed by a bang behind my chair.

Apparently they had all heard it but had thought nothing of it. Perhaps such noises were an everyday occurrence in their circle. 'If you say it happened behind your chair,' Mr Bull nodded, 'we'll investigate.'

Sure enough, flat on the floor behind my chair was the framed portrait of a Red Indian that had apparently fallen off the wall, except that the picture hook was still on the wall and the string behind the frame was still intact. Mr Bull explained that he had a Red Indian helper – Sitting Bull, I wondered irreverently? – and that the portrait was a psychic drawing by one of the circle who had seen his guide.

He dismissed the affair as of no significance, but logical Doris had to ask for an explanation. 'Possibly the guide's very happy you've joined our circle,' somebody volunteered, but that was not good enough for me. I had had little experience at that time of unusual physical happenings. I knew it was no trick, but I just could not explain it.

We were then served with tea and biscuits. 'How did you enjoy the meeting?' somebody asked me. 'Enjoy' struck me as a curious way to describe my feelings. 'Very nice, thank you,' I replied non-committally, in my childish way, all the while thinking that they were a weird bunch and that I would not return.

I did not of course discuss the matter with my parents,

but I told Marcia Clasper that I was scared to go back. She expressed the view that I had not given the circle a fair chance. 'Once is not enough,' she said.

I spent all the next week deciding not to return, and then at the last minute I went along again. The preliminaries were very similar to those the time before. Mr Bull asked us to meditate and told us we were safe, that we were protected from danger. On this occasion I felt very drowsy and I must have drifted off to sleep. I remembered nothing more until Mr Bull shook me and said, 'Come along, Doris, raise yourself. I'm putting on the light.'

The other members of the circle seemed to be studying me curiously. 'Do you know what happened?' Mr Bull asked. 'You've been in what we call a trance.'

I had heard the word before, but had never thought that I would go into one; in my simple way I believed that one had to be hypnotized to enter into such a state. Nor had I ever seen anyone in a trance, to the best of my knowledge.

They then told me that my sister Emmie had spoken to the circle through me. She had given her name, and said she was happy to use me as a medium to talk to them but that I was far too young to develop my precious gift. I was not, she told them, to sit in the circle any more; I had to learn to deal with life first, but later I would go all over the world, using the special gifts that I had.

I remembered Mrs Clasper's similar words to me, and I was dreadfully disappointed that Emmie wanted me to leave the circle just when I was becoming interested in it. Mr Bull said that Emmie had told them that she had achieved her purpose; she had made contact with me. She would protect me and try to guide my life so that I could do the work that I had come into this world to do.

This was not of course the first time that Emmie had manifested herself to me or through me, and I found this curious because I had never been very close to her during her lifetime. As a little child, I had felt that she was somebody very special, and there was a quality about her that always shone. My main impression of her was that she was very beautiful; she had a beauty of spirit as well as a beautiful face, but she was so much older than I was and therefore rather remote. Now I did not want to heed her advice. 'I don't think I'll take any notice of that,' I said cheerily. 'I want to come back.' I was enjoying a sense of achievement. I was progressing fast. I had already experienced the state of trance, which was more than some of the others had done!

But they refused to have me, and so I left the circle, but inwardly I was determined to explore matters further.

Life soon had other attractions for me, however, and it was not long before I fell in love and got married, as I have related. I was too busy being a married woman and a young mother to concern myself seriously with spiritualism, but I maintained my friendships with people who mixed in psychic circles and I attended a number of meetings, all the time learning and adding to my experience. Nothing very dramatic happened to me at that time, at least nothing worth recording. Fortunately I was married to a man who never laughed at me, indeed who believed in my gifts and who allowed me a certain freedom to exploit them.

It was after the birth of Brian that I started seriously to develop my other gift as a spiritual healer. I had met a number of people who were healers and who were convinced that I was similarly gifted; they persuaded me to join them in their work. Mr Jenkins was an experienced healer at Ilford Spiritualist Church, and he invited me to study with him for a year, offering to guide and help me. I became his novice.

We met once a week in the evening and worked from six o'clock until half past ten. There were about a dozen healers in our group, and the same large hall that served as the place of worship on Sundays was our consulting room. The healers worked in a ring, and the patients sat on chairs, waiting to be called. We had a secretary who made appointments and who kept the case histories.

The patients came in all shapes and sizes, and our group often saw as many as a hundred in any one evening. Some had been recommended to us by local doctors who had done as much as they could for their patients but who felt that they might benefit from the help we could give them. I even had doctors come to me for treatment! Very many patients, particularly elderly ones, came because they felt that their regular doctors could do no more for them; they were hoping for a miracle and we were their last possibility, as they thought.

Healers do not necessarily have any medical knowledge and they have rarely had any medical training. They do not claim to replace the medical profession, but rather to supplement the wonderful work of qualified medical practitioners. Where appropriate, they will refer a patient to a doctor. All they can do – all they seek to do – is to offer help.

Help can come in many forms – it is sometimes physical, such as by touching, or it can be mental, such as in giving comfort. Increasingly the medical profession has come to recognize the potential value to a patient of spiritual healing.

I started as Mr Jenkins's assistant, but even before my probationary year was over, I was achieving worthwhile results on my own. Later I achieved what some people regarded as miraculous results, but this was after practising my art (or my gift, whatever it should be called) for many years. Mr Jenkins taught me only so much, and I developed my own technique, almost by instinct. As I grew more experienced, so my ratio of success increased. I healed every week for many years.

30

I have come to believe that mental frustration can be as dangerous to health as a recognizable disease. Seemingly healthy people who are frustrated with their lives or who undergo tremendous mental conflict can create an imbalance in their body structure, sometimes leading to cancer for instance. In such cases, the healing I have done is not unlike that, I suppose, of a psychiatrist.

Most people who have come to me for healing, however, have been suffering from such things as backache, joint problems, headaches, internal pains – or perhaps they have been partially crippled and found difficulty in walking. Sometimes, I know, they have not believed that I can help them, and they have been nervous, but they have come because someone has asked them to as a last try. 'Doris,' they may say, 'I've got this terrible back. I've been everywhere and I can't get any help.'

'I'll do what I can to help you,' I say. 'Will you sit down?'

I then usually touch the patient. I had been taught by Mr Jenkins to touch where I felt guided to go, but I almost always start by touching the patient's hands. This usually relaxes him or her. I have been told that I have a calming voice, but the calming effect is accelerated by touch. I will then often touch the patient's head, followed by his back, or wherever my instinct tells me to touch.

I am not sure how my touch affects the patient, but I know of course what I feel. The Chinese speak of yin and yang, the positive and the negative forces. I am naturally right-handed, and I believe that I have positive force in my right hand, by which I mean that I sometimes feel power emanating from it; rarely from my left hand, where negative force operates. When I touch a patient, I sometimes feel a sort of electric current between my right hand and his or her body; I can also feel tremendous heat or great cold on occasion.

Difficult as it is to explain, I sometimes feel colours

coming from my right hand, and it is interesting to note in this context that several patients have told me that they have seen colours radiating from me while I have been treating them. Nowadays I heal quite often by the conscious use of colour because I have come to realize what an important therapeutic role colour plays in our lives. At its most basic, certain colours are restful and have a tranquillizing effect, whereas others are violent.

As proof that I do not regard spiritual healing as a substitute for normal medical attention I cite the case of my own son Brian. It became clear to my husband and me soon after the baby's birth that there was something very wrong with him, and our doctor was treating him for stomach trouble. He was eighteen months old – at about the time when I had just completed my apprenticeship with Mr Jenkins – when the Great Ormond Street Hospital diagnosed his problem. No wonder the local GP had been getting nowhere, for Brian had a rare illness which required a special diet of bananas and gluten-free bread made from soya beans. But this was in the middle of a war, and bananas were a very scarce commodity, even on the black market. The British Red Cross came to the rescue, and every month, thanks to them, ten pounds of bananas reached us from South Africa.

I tried to bring up Brian as a normal child, and I explained to him that he had a disability with which he had to learn to live. Although he had the pallid look of other sufferers from his unusual illness, thank God his growth was not stunted, as was often the case, so I was told.

In all other respects Brian was indeed a normal boy, and he adjusted well to the situation, as I had taught and urged him to do. I never thought of trying to heal him myself, except insofar as I was trying to create for him living conditions in which he could prosper – which is no more than every good parent does.

He was thirteen when I first had the idea that he might benefit from visiting our clinic, and I put the thought to him. 'What's the point?' he amused me by replying, 'I can have you at home any time.'

'Oh, no,' I said, 'I wouldn't think of healing you myself. I thought you might go to one of the other healers.'

Brian agreed to go along, and I made an appointment for him through the secretary. However, the healer to whom Brian had been assigned was himself taken ill that night, and Brian was transferred to me! I think probably I would not have accepted him as a patient had I not been working at the time with another healer as part of a team. There was at least another independent person to deal with my son, the patient.

While the other healer held Brian's hands and touched him on the head and stomach, I felt impelled to touch his neck. The treatment (or, as I usually call it, the healing) did not last very long. There was no obvious change in Brian and he went home. This was just before nine o'clock.

I myself got home about two hours later to be greeted by my husband on the doorstep. He was very alarmed.

'What have you done to our son?' he demanded, almost angrily.

'Nothing,' I replied. 'What on earth do you mean? I only touched him on the neck, as I felt impelled.'

'Go up and have a look,' Jack said.

I ran into Brian's bedroom, where he lay on the bed. His neck was grossly swollen. I was frankly terrified and could not think how my contact with his neck could possibly have produced this result. And then my son accused me: 'You did it,' he said. 'When you touched my neck, I felt a very funny feeling. Now look at me.'

I felt awful, and for the first time asked myself whether I was right to try to heal. Was I perhaps dabbling in something I did not understand, exercising some power I could not control? Why was it that my only problem as a healer should have arisen in the case of my own flesh and blood?

We sent at once for the doctor, who diagnosed glandular fever and rushed Brian to hospital, where he was given an immediate blood transfusion. The following day we were told that he might have leukaemia. Needless to say we were distraught, and I remember thinking that Brian was our only son and I could have no other children. I felt desperately miserable for the poor boy, and I was asking myself all the time whether in some strange way I was responsible for his condition. He had been perfectly all right apparently until I had touched his neck, but surely a little thing like that could not have induced leukaemia? It was ridiculous to suppose so, and yet it had resulted in a horribly swollen neck.

As I was leaving his bedside, Brian looked at me. His eyes were pleading, no longer accusing. 'Mummy,' he said, 'let me have your hanky. I want to put it under my pillow because it smells of you.' I now know that this was his way of trying to keep contact with me. I knew at the time that his request meant that he loved me, and I felt much happier.

No sooner had he spoken than I heard a voice. It told me that my son did not have leukaemia, or any fatal illness for that matter. I told the doctor so, although I did not tell him how I knew.

'Have you any medical knowledge?' he asked.

'None at all,' I replied, because I did not think that my work as a healer was what he had in mind.

'So why do you say you know your son is not suffering from leukaemia?' he said, looking at me with a certain respect, as if my tone of voice had sounded convincing.

'I had a feeling,' was all I could say.

He looked at me again and nodded. 'Do you know the value of prayer?' he enquired.

I was on surer ground here. Prayer is potent, positive thought. 'Yes, I most certainly do,' I replied.

'Then if I were you,' said the doctor, 'I'd go home and pray that you're right.'

I am no fair-weather prayer of prayers. I have always prayed. This time I made the following commitment to God: 'If you save the life of my only son, whatever else I do in this world I will always heal the sick.'

Today Brian, although still somewhat pallid in complexion, is a strapping fellow of six foot three. He is a former Marine commando and is now a chief fire officer. He still has occasional attacks that put him back on soya-flour bread, but my voice was right when even the doctors were in doubt. No one ever discovered what was the matter with him when his neck swelled, but it was certainly neither glandular fever nor leukaemia.

What the doctors were certain about is that his blood count was so low when he arrived in hospital that had he not been given a blood transfusion within twenty-four hours, nobody could have saved him. If Brian's neck had not become enlarged as the result of my touching it, he would not have gone to hospital and had the transfusion. My healing power, which had seemed in this instance to be a destructive force, had turned out to be a means to an end. It may have saved my son's life. It was a healing power after all.

To this day I have kept my promise to heal the sick. It is a function that I regard as perhaps my most important in life.

# Chapter Four

When I tell people that I have been married three times,
they usually seem surprised. That I have twice been
divorced is a matter of some astonishment even to myself.
But facts are facts and I cannot get away from them. The
circumstances were however very unusual. I am happily
married now to my present – and I am sure my last –
husband, and for a long time I was happily married also to
the others.

I have always been a great believer in the institution of
marriage and in the importance of the family unit. I had the
example of my parents' happy marriage to guide me, and
no one can have seen greater evidence of the love that two
people can have for each other than someone like myself
who has observed at first hand the love that extends beyond
the grave.

A particular example comes to mind. Late one morning –
it must have been in 1950 or thereabouts – I was busy
dusting the house when, as clear as can be, I saw the
Reverend Albury from St Mary's Church in South Woodford, who had died some time previously. He appeared
before me in the house and told me to go to the London
Zoo. I hesitated at first, not unnaturally, but the more I
thought about the message, the more I felt impelled to obey
it.

I told my husband that I had a feeling that I had to go
into town. He must have been used to my feelings since he
did not seem at all surprised when after lunch I changed my
clothes and left the house. It was after three o'clock when I
reached Regent's Park, and I decided that the first thing I

wanted to do, before even seeing the animals, was to have a cup of tea. So I went into the Zoo's restaurant.

A woman was sitting at the next table whom I did not at first recognize because she was wearing a big hat that hid her face. When she turned to me, I saw that it was Mrs Albury, widow of the Reverend Albury who was responsible for my presence there.

'Doris, what on earth are you doing here?' she said.

'I might well ask you the same question,' I replied.

Mrs Albury was an Australian and, following the death of her husband, she was intending shortly to return to the country of her birth. 'I've come here,' she told me, 'to say goodbye to England.' Apparently she and her late husband had first met at the Zoo and it had been an important meeting-place for them before their marriage.

I knew then that I had to tell her that her husband had sent me to her. She did not doubt me but she asked me what it meant. I was able to tell her that her husband was only dead in the physical sense, that his life had not ended and that, in sending me to see her, he was indicating that he would try to protect her wherever she was – and above all that he loved her dearly.

No doubt theirs was one of the perfect relationships, and there are probably many more than people think, even in this age of easy divorce.

I have to confess that my own first marriage became very much less than perfect. I am inhibited to some extent in discussing the failure of my marriage by the fact that Jack was the father of my son, and I have never explained to Brian why I left his father or why I made up my mind to do so within twenty-four hours after sixteen years of marriage. There are in any case certain matters that should, I believe, remain confidential between husband and wife.

Since it is the fashion nowadays to tell all, and since indiscreet revelation seems to be required of an author, I

37

hope I may be forgiven if I concentrate on Jack's short-comings and ignore his many good qualities. How else can I explain my own conduct? It took me two years to discover that my husband was a drinker and a gambler, but that did not greatly worry me. I was more concerned that, as our marriage progressed, I began to feel that he was no longer a good companion. He was not really a home man and often, when we went together to the cinema, he would leave in the middle of the programme, go to the pub next door and meet me outside when the film was over.

Had that been all, I would probably have remained his wife until his death in 1974. But unfortunately I came to realize that my husband was weak, certainly about financial matters. He was a shockingly bad manager, financially unreliable, and the time came when he put me in a position that I found untenable. I will not say more. The nature of the straw that broke the camel's back must remain a secret between us, but I hasten to say that Jack was never dishonest and it is right too to point out that he was always a good father to Brian and Margaret.

We were divorced in 1954, shortly before Brian's four-teenth birthday; Margaret was then nine years old. I married my second husband, Richard Collins, almost exactly two years later. Dick was about fifteen years younger than Jack and much nearer my own age. I had first met him when he brought his wife to me for healing. They lived in Ilford and had heard about my work. She died nine months later of cancer. I knew I could not save her life because she was in a terminal condition when I first saw her, but I hope and believe that I gave her some relief and some peace. The three of us became firm friends, and I visited them at least once a week. Curiously her name was Doris too and their elder son was also named Brian; they had a second child, little Richard, who was a dwarf.

As she was dying, Mrs Collins said to me: 'Doris, look

after Richard for me.' I knew that she meant her dwarf son and not her husband, who shared the same name. This was my main reason for keeping in touch with the family after the mother's death. I invited them home and, somewhat to my surprise, Dick made it clear that he did not approve of the atmosphere in which I appeared to him to be living, and in particular he expressed the view that Jack was not a suitable husband for me.

Although I had my own ideas on that subject, I rather resented Dick's criticism until I began to realize that he was genuinely concerned for me. I suppose I knew in my heart that he was falling in love with me, especially when he said one day, 'Any time you want to leave Jack, you can always have a home with us.' But I was not about to be disloyal to Jack while I remained married to him.

It was about a year later that I finally left Jack. He begged me to return, but I refused. I took Margaret and went to stay with Dick and his mother. There were six of us in the house – Dick, his mother, his two children, Margaret and me – and I had no option but to leave Brian with his father for the time being, although he spent a lot of his time with us.

My marriage to Richard Collins, who incidentally was Passenger Manager of the Italian General Shipping Line, was a watershed in my life. I married him in 1956, and it was at this time that I began seriously to involve myself in the spiritualist movement. I became a very active member of the movement at almost exactly the time I became Doris Collins, the name by which I am known professionally to this day. The next three years were incredibly hectic.

It had become increasingly obvious to me that, in addition to my gift as a healer, I had powers of clair-voyance and clairaudience. Clairvoyance involves seeing the past and the future, and clairaudience is of course hearing voices. I was curious to know more about these

39

gifts, and also to develop them. I sat with several mediums for this purpose, for apart from my own curiosity, I wanted to teach others what I was beginning to find out about myself. I should perhaps say, for the sake of the uninitiated, that a medium is a channel between two states of existence. If that is a somewhat difficult concept, perhaps I can liken a medium to a television set that picks up vibrations from the ether and presents them in a material form to the viewer.

At any rate I sought out people whom I hoped could help me to understand myself. I asked one particularly famous lady why and how certain 'gifts' worked. She merely replied, 'One day, Doris, you'll learn and understand.' This was not very helpful, and my logical and practical mind felt that there must be a better explanation. I now realize that she did not know the answer.

It would be supremely arrogant on my part to claim that I now know the answer myself, but I shall have more to say about this later. I began to wonder however whether I did not know more about the psychic gift than many of the people from whom I was making enquiries. It occurred to me that, having run healing circles successfully for some time, I might usefully also start teaching circles. It may have been a little bit like the blind leading the blind, but I believe I achieved some useful results. People came to me who had seen me work or heard me lecture, and I discovered that, in involving myself in other people's problems and interests, I was learning a great deal myself. I once picked a woman out of the audience who sat with me for three or four years until I had to give up the circle. Today she is a well-known medium.

I was on surer ground when it came to healing. One of my pupils – if that is the right word – was Sid Staples. When I first met him in 1951 he did not believe in spiritualism. His wife was an invalid at the time, and he

40

used to bring her to see me at her insistence. While I was giving her healing, he always sat outside in the car. One day I went outside to talk to him about his wife. As we shook hands, I knew he had healing ability, and I told him so. He laughed at me, as if to indicate that he thought this was so much rubbish. But as he saw the improvement in his wife, he became interested in my work and he asked me whether I would like to train him as a healer. I gladly seized the opportunity. He was an excellent trainee and went from strength to strength, so much so that in 1957 he became Organizing Secretary of the National (now International) Federation of Spiritual Healers.

I myself was later honoured by being made Vice-President of the Union of Spiritual Mediums (now called the Institute of Spiritualist Mediums). They are not a trade union in the ordinary sense, but rather an organization of people who believe in psychic power as a beneficent force. I have been linked with them almost since their inception. In 1958 I was asked to become President of the Woodford National Spiritualist Church, the church that I had first visited as a girl. I remained President for over five years, and in 1981 when the church was rebuilt I was chosen to take the first service, and I have never ceased to have some connection with it.

I was never busier or more active in the spiritualist world than in the years immediately following my second marriage. At one time I actually had engagements three years ahead! It was at this time that I first practised absent healing, or healing at a distance. I often now give healing over the telephone, and I have frequently dealt with 'patients' over the air when I have appeared on radio programmes. Part of the technique is to make recipients aware that they can help themselves. Healing is not only the laying on of hands. It is also one soul speaking to another, giving courage and confidence.

41

My dear friend Michael Bentine, who knows more about the paranormal than most people, telephoned me one day to say that he had just received a message from Pretoria in South Africa that his brother-in-law had been taken so seriously ill that little hope was held out for his recovery. 'Will you join us?' he asked. 'We'll sit down and send healing.' Michael is one of the sanest, most down-to-earth men you could possibly meet, and he certainly thought the exercise was worthwhile.

At an agreed time, Michael in his house and I in mine sat down and prayed simultaneously. I had been to South Africa and although I did not know the house where Michael's brother-in-law lived, I knew the location and so could visualize the actual place. This helped me to send out healing powers. I must have concentrated for about fifteen minutes. Two days later Michael reported that there had been a remarkable improvement in his brother-in-law's condition.

I met the man's wife one year later in England. She told me that her husband had described me accurately, although he had never seen or heard of me at the time. When she had gone in to see her husband the following day after our absent healing, he had said: 'A large lady with a round face came in and took my hand and said, "You're going to get better, you know." I asked the nursing staff who she was. They told me she didn't exist, that I must have been dreaming.' The wife questioned her husband further, and apparently he described me exactly. I was convinced that I had projected my image into his mind.

This was some time later than the events I am currently relating. I had never been abroad when I married Richard. It was in 1960 that I went to the West Indies for the first time, beginning the long series of foreign travel that was to become such a feature of my life. But first I went to Scotland, and for someone who had barely set foot out of

42

the London area, it was almost as great an adventure as going to Trinidad.

I was asked by the Union of Spiritualist Mediums to tour England and Scotland for two weeks on their behalf, to demonstrate clairvoyance. This entailed driving up to Inverness and back. I was not the most experienced driver in those days and I drove alone through the night. There was a terrible storm just before I reached Crieff, so I pulled into a lay-by and dozed off. I was awoken by the heavy lorries in the early hours and I set off on the last part of my journey north at six o'clock in the morning. There was practically no traffic on the lonely road. I seemed to be completely alone in the mountains, with the little streams running down the mountainsides. Only the singing birds kept me company. I felt exhilarated, and I got out of the car and breathed in the wonderful Scottish air and atmosphere. I felt at one with all life.

I stayed in Inverness with the couple who had arranged my meetings in Scotland. They had received a letter for me. It was from a Church of Scotland clergyman, and it upset me dreadfully. I was, he wrote, a very evil woman, defying God's laws in practising my gift. He knew that when I died, my soul would burn in the hellfires of damnation!

Everyone in the public eye is used to receiving fan letters and hate letters, but this from a man of God was peculiarly hurtful. Was he unaware of Jesus's admonition to 'Love ye one another'? How could a man love his God and wish to destroy his neighbour?

I believe that the path a man treads is his own business, but how he treats his brothers is God's business. I also believe that as you sow, so you must reap – usually in this life, but if not in this life, certainly at some time in another existence.

I have made many mistakes in life. Who has not? But I have never led an evil life. I have tried always to help people in need, and I determined there and then that, notwithstanding ignorant criticism, I would use the gifts that God had given me, come what may.

# Chapter Five

o◯oo◯oo◯o

It was while I was in Scotland that my husband telephoned
to say that he had received a message from the West Indies.
Apparently at some time I had given a sitting to a
government minister from that part of the world. I had
forgotten all about it.

That is not as strange as it may seem. Once I have dealt
psychically with a problem, I usually put it right out of my
mind. People who visit me more than once are sometimes
surprised that I do not always remember what I told them
before. I find that this is the only way in which I can
function successfully. When I am working, I am concentrating on the matter in hand. It then becomes a thing of the
past and there has to be some special reason for me to recall
it. I do not have to go into a trance to see things, but my
memory of them is often no better than if I had been in one.

So the fact that I did not remember my distinguished
visitor should cause no surprise. I see so many people, and
while I am working they are all alike to me. It seems
however that I must have helped the gentleman enormously
because he recommended me to the attention of a very close
friend in Trinidad, and this man had come to England
specially to see me.

Although I sent out notices of meetings, I never advertised for customers, if that is the right word for the different
people who came to me for help or with their problems –
one of the most common being how to contact loved ones
they had lost. A sort of bush telegraph operated, but I was
surprised that its message had reached the Caribbean. I
found also that, while I neither sought nor avoided pub-

licity, my name was beginning to appear in the press – and not just in local newspapers.

In the previous year, for example, an appeal had been put out over the radio for someone to adopt a blind labrador. Animals have always been important to me and to my family, and we already had a golden labrador named Bessie. Unknown to me, my stepson Brian telephoned the *Daily Mirror* and told them that I would be able to provide the ideal home for the blind animal. He told them that I was a healer, that I had cured Bessie of hardpad and that she had later had twelve puppies.

Although there were over a hundred applicants, I was chosen to look after the blind creature, and I found myself in the national newspapers, much to my amusement and surprise, as if I had done some wonderful feat like climbing Mount Everest or crossing Niagara Falls in a barrel. Perhaps the story was copied by the newspapers in the West Indies, but locally at any rate I could not go anywhere without exciting comment. I kept the dog until he died. I did indeed heal him and he recovered some of his sight. I bought a large double chain, and Bessie took him everywhere she went.

There never was a dog like Bessie, as far as I was concerned. She was one of the reasons I did not like travelling, because she often became ill when I went away. There was an amazing rapport between us and she was very attached to the children. They were brought up with a knowledge of what I did, and they accepted my work as natural. Bessie, however, when occasionally I went into a trance at a development circle, would howl in another room. She was almost human, or as human as a dog can be. I taught her to laugh. 'Bessie, laugh,' I would say, and she would bare her teeth and make a bark-like snarl. I have to admit she looked terrifying when she laughed and she once frightened the postman, who mistook her laugh for something more threatening.

I have had quite a lot of dogs in my time, but Bessie is the only one I ever see. She will often turn up just for a minute. More than one person in an audience has told me, 'Do you know there was a dog sitting at your feet on the platform?' Bessie of course died some years ago, but she is still with me.

But to get back to the West Indies. Shortly after the telephone call to my husband while I was in Scotland – in fact almost immediately after my return home – the doorbell rang. I was cleaning the house at the time and had made no appointments to see anybody. Two West Indian gentlemen were standing there. 'We've come to take you back,' one of them said.

'Take me back? Where?' I enquired.

'To the West Indies,' the other one said, as matter-of-factly as if he meant the West India Dock Road in London's East End.

I thought at first that they were joking, and I was almost petrified when I realized that they were deadly serious and wanted me to leave then and there. I thought in my confusion of saying that I could not go because I had not finished the housework, or because my hair was not properly done, or that I was unsuitably dressed. Eventually I plucked up courage and insisted that I had no intention of going anywhere.

When it became obvious that they did not intend to kidnap me, I invited them in. They told me that they had come on the recommendation of the government minister I had previously seen. It appears that I had told him that the Leader of the Opposition in Trinidad and Tobago was a sick man and that healing would help him. As they spoke to me, I began to remember my earlier visitor, but I could certainly not remember having discussed, or even heard of, the Leader of the Opposition – Dr Rudranath Capildeo.

This distinguished politician had become an almost

helpless invalid. He had had two attacks of rheumatic fever which had damaged his heart. I was told that he had expressed the view that he had reached the end of the line, but he had no idea that his friends were coming to me as a last resort.

They put a first-class return air ticket on the table. I am not sure that I had ever seen one. I told them I could not possibly leave my home to fly across the world, but they begged me to change my mind. They would put up in a local hotel for two days while I spoke to my husband and reconsidered the matter.

Having spoken to Richard, I telephoned them to say that I could afford to be away for three days, but when they pointed out that I would be travelling for the best part of two days there and back – I must have been very naive not to have realized this – I consented to a week.

We stopped first in Tobago before going on to Port of Spain, and I thought I would die. The place was like an oven and I wondered whether I could possibly work in such heat. In Port of Spain I was met by an official of Dr Capildeo's political party who took me to the house of a charming English couple where it had been arranged I would stay. Two hours later I was picked up and taken to see Dr Capildeo.

I think we must both have been confused. I had never flown before and after such a long flight might well have been suffering from jet-lag, yet I was put straight to work. As for him, he soon made it clear that had he known earlier who and what I was, he would not have agreed to see me, let alone have encouraged me to cross the Atlantic for the purpose.

He was a Hindu and represented broadly the Chinese and Indian sections of the community. The leader of the government party was supported by the majority African section. I found Dr Capildeo sitting on the porch of the

48

house to which I was taken. He rose and introduced himself, shaking my hand. I had the curious sensation, for the first time ever although I have had similar experiences many times since, that I had known him all my life. He was no stranger.

'You're Doris Collins,' he said. 'I don't believe in what you do and had I known they were sending for you, I would have stopped it.' Despite his words, he spoke warmly and graciously. 'But please come in,' he added, 'and perhaps sit and have a cup of tea.'

We sat on a settee and talked. I felt unusually clairvoyant and I pretty well told him the story of his life, as if indeed I had known him all that time. I had made no enquiries about him – knowing too much about somebody can actually inhibit me – and I think he realized that my gift was genuine, particularly when I spoke about his unsuccessful marriage and his struggle to be a politician. Tears began to flow down his cheeks.

'I find it absolutely incredible,' he told me, 'that you should know so much about me without ever having met me or heard of me before.' Little did he know that barely a week earlier I could not even have said with certainty where the West Indies were! Later he was to tell me that he too felt we had always known each other. 'Perhaps you'll let me give you some healing,' was all I could say in reply.

He agreed readily, telling me that he had been given only six months to live and that he had not been out of the house for many weeks.

I gave him healing every day I was there, and before I left, believe it or not, he was driving me around his beautiful island. This was one of the most spectacular and instant successes I had ever achieved. 'You have given me a new lease of life,' he said as he saw me off to England. I felt that by that time we were already firm friends.

49

I returned to the West Indies twice at Rudy Capildeo's request. I was beginning to understand that I had to operate not just locally at home, but also in the wider world. I remembered the words of Mrs Clasper: 'You have the great power of healing. You'll go all over the world using this power.' In one sense I was never away from Trinidad because Rudy used frequently to telephone me for advice on political matters. Amazingly, although I am not a particularly political person, I felt able to advise him, and I gave him constant absent healing. He paid a wonderful tribute to me, telling journalists that I had succeeded in helping to restore his health when others could do little. Soon after my first visit, he had carried out what he called 'a difficult and dangerous campaign', addressing as many as half a dozen meetings in one evening.

The last time I went out was just before the elections in Trinidad and Tobago. The actual date had not yet been set but it was presumed that they would take place on a particular day. As soon as I arrived at the airport, more than one person asked me when voting day would be, and I said the first date that came into my head. This was reported in the press, along with the comment that my suggestion would prove incorrect because it was not a logical date at all. In fact the presumed day was changed and I was proved right. Thereafter I could do no wrong.

On this visit Rudy was seemingly fit and well and very active politically. He was looking forward to attending the forthcoming Trinidad Independence Conference at Marlborough House in London, but first he had to campaign. He asked me to join him, saying that he felt it would help him to have me along. He had an official driver but sometimes I drove for him. We stopped at little villages where we were invariably welcomed and fed.

One night, while I was driving, the steering failed and the car went out of control. We fell off the road into a field of

50

sugar-cane. Rudy had been sitting with me in the front; his sister and niece were in the back. The car was a total wreck. This was a terrible experience for us all, but particularly for the two of us in the front seats. Rudy went through the windscreen and somehow I got hold of him and pulled him back. His most serious injuries were a broken patella and a broken left humerus. I felt as though I had exploded and I could hardly breathe. My ribs were fractured and flying glass had cut a hole in my knee.

Within minutes we were surrounded by people and rushed to hospital, where Rudy was operated on by a French surgeon. I woke to find my ribs strapped up. The pain in my body was so great that I could not even reach for a glass of water.

Rudy was far more badly injured than I was, and just as soon as I was able, I went to his bedside. The nurses had told him that his recovery would be slow and that he would not be able to go to London for the conference that meant so much to him. 'Nonsense,' I said, 'you'll go there all right.' I practically crawled into his room every day and, with the full approval of the medical staff, gave him healing. He made a remarkable recovery.

He never tired of telling people that his recovery was the combined result of orthodox surgery and spiritual healing. 'I am convinced,' he said, 'that the healing Doris Collins practises is a perfectly natural phenomenon and that its basic principles can be described in modern-day scientific language which should be acceptable to all seekers of truth unburdened by prejudice.'

Dr Capildeo had degrees both in science and philosophy, so perhaps his opinion is to be respected. He was duly able to attend the Independence Conference, although still a member of the opposition party, and he took part in every session. He died many years later in England from a kidney complaint. He never got into power, but for a man who had been given only six months to live, he certainly led a full and exciting life for a long time beyond his own expectation. He had a Hindu funeral in south London, and I was honoured to take part in the ceremony.

# Chapter Six

oᴑooᴑooᴑo

When I returned from the West Indies for the third time, in 1961 following the car accident, I became quite ill. Everybody told me that I was trying to do too much. I was doing full-time psychic and healing work as well as running a household, and I was having a very difficult time with my husband Richard, as I shall explain.

My doctor advised me to give up the sort of work that was never finished. It would be better, he said, if I had an ordinary nine-to-five job that would be less demanding and less wearing on my mind and body. I was determined never wholly to give up helping other people where I could, and particularly never entirely to abandon my healing, but I saw some sense in what my doctor and many friends advised. I could always fit in my psychic and healing work on a part-time basis, perhaps on Sundays and once a week in the evening.

It was while I was on the plane returning from Trinidad that an idea for a more conventional occupation was put to me. I found myself seated next to a woman who worked in advertising and she told me that I would make an excellent interviewer for a market research company. This field of endeavour was entirely new to me and I just filed the idea in the back of my mind, although I mentioned the conversation to my family. They too had long been urging me to discontinue, or cut down on, my psychic work, which they felt drew too much energy from me. It was certainly too depleting when I was below par following the accident.

It was not long afterwards that I saw a job advertised for an interviewer for the Nestlé Company. I at once remembered the woman on the plane, and I read this as a sign. So I applied for the job and was in no way surprised when I landed it. The beauty of it was that I was employed as a freelance, so my time was very much my own. Within three months however I was invited to join the full-time staff on a monthly salary.

I confess that I loved the job. It entailed getting out and about and talking to people, something that I was well qualified to do. My health improved dramatically as soon as I left the house and met the public. So perhaps my family and friends had not been wrong in advising me to give up full-time psychic work.

It was not long before I was made Area Controller for East London and the East Coast. As such, I had to supervise about forty women interviewers, allocate and check on their work, and attend conferences. The company put an Answerphone in my home. I worked from the house and went to the City office once a week at first, and twice a week later. The job also required a lot of driving. After two years I was appointed Administrative Controller for London and the South and East Coasts.

Unfortunately, however, my success did not please Richard. I had not told him that I was replying to the advertisement, and when I gave him the news that I had got the job, instead of congratulating me, he said nothing. I can see now that he was jealous. Everything I did seemed to work, whereas everything he did seemed suddenly to go wrong.

It was at least two years after my second marriage before I realized that my new husband had a very difficult mental problem. It began to manifest itself gradually, and I had had no idea at all about it when I agreed to marry him. He was outwardly a most charming man and perfectly normal with other people, but to his family, his obsessive behaviour was most tiresome. He had his regular pattern of life which

54

nothing was permitted to disturb. Everything had to be done at a certain time and in a certain way. After wiping dishes, the teacloth had to be placed in a particular way, for example; his breakfast tray had to be laid in a certain manner, the cup and saucer always in the same position. His routine hardly ever varied.

I tried to make light of these minor peculiarities – of his excessive precision and tidiness. He insisted on cleaning his own shoes and then shaving every night at nine o'clock, in preparation for the morning. On one occasion I tried to jolly him out of his routine by singing (to the tune of 'Who's Afraid of the Big Bad Wolf?') some words that came into my head: 'Wash and shave and clean our shoes, clean our shoes, clean our shoes; wash and shave and clean our shoes, all ready for the morning.' He merely smiled.

He was also extremely pedantic, but these little things did not greatly concern me. I felt I could easily put up with them, even his long silences. We once drove to the coast and he said not a word the whole journey.

'What's wrong?' I eventually asked him.

'Nothing,' he replied.

'Why don't you talk?' I went on.

'Small talk is gossip,' he said, 'and I don't believe in gossip.'

I was far more concerned with a more sinister streak in his behaviour. Our garden had to be like a park and the children were not allowed to play there. I used however to let them do so when he went to work, until he started setting little traps to see if his wishes were being defied.

Richard soon began to imagine that he had physical problems; I do not think he ever considered at that time that his problems might be mental. He had a chip on his shoulder about the world and its inhabitants. Everybody was trying to do him down. There was nobody he could trust. More than once he went to hospital with an imaginary complaint, only to be sent home. I tried to give him healing but he was not the best subject. He preferred on these occasions to lie in bed all day – sometimes all weekend – saying he felt tired. He often became very depressed, and then very aggressive – though not, I hasten to say, towards the children.

His aggression towards a new boss precipitated his mental deterioration. He had always enjoyed a great deal of autonomy in his position, which was one of some importance. The crunch came during an office party to which I had not been invited as it was a strictly business affair.

Richard told me he wasn't going to stand any more nonsense from his new boss, and psychically I foresaw disaster. I felt unable to go to bed before his return, and I was working myself up into something of a state when he telephoned me. 'Will you please bring the car and come and get me?' was all he said.

When eventually I reached his office, very early in the morning, he was waiting outside with his own typewriter in his hands. I never understood why he insisted on having it at work when there were plenty of office machines.

The assistant manager told me that my husband had attacked his boss and that members of the staff had walked Richard round the streets in an attempt to placate him. Richard's story was that he had not actually assaulted the man. He had, he said, gone into a little office to talk to him and, in the course of conversation, had poked him. His boss however claimed that he had been attacked physically. He had dismissed Richard on the spot.

I drove him home, made him a cup of tea, and we went to bed. There was no point in talking to Dick, who most of the time was crying with anger. I was desperate and had to treat the problem as an emergency. I decided to go to head office in Genoa, so I booked a plane and arrived in Italy the following day. The morning after my arrival, I presented

56

myself unannounced at the headquarters of the Italian Shipping Line when the doors opened at eight o'clock.

I was received with wonderful old-world Italian politeness by two officers of the company. I think they must have been impressed as well as surprised that an Englishwoman who spoke no Italian should have flown out to plead for her husband. I soon learnt however that my husband's reputation had preceded me. They had received reports from London for some time past about his alleged difficult behaviour and about supposed peculiarities in his method of working. I asked them to elaborate and they spoke about him being very pedantic. I knew all too well what they meant, and I felt the ground giving way beneath me. I would be unable to save Dick's job.

I pointed out somewhat pathetically that he would lose his pension – there were no redundancy payments in those days – and the men looked at me kindly and said they would consider the matter, but they could not override the decision of the man on the spot. In the end Dick got a little golden handshake, if golden is the right word for about £600. But as to the job, that was lost forever.

Richard had been a Regimental Sergeant Major in the Army, and he liked authority. We all had to jump to his orders, and on one occasion I had complained to him that he was seeking to run his home like an Army camp. I remember saying, 'You can't be an RSM at home.' Although he soon found a small job with another shipping company, it was not a position of importance, and in fact he never again held a position of authority. This preyed on his mind, and was, I believe, what accelerated his decline.

He would take days off from work and just lie around the house and cry. I could not help him very much because he would not allow me to try. He was aggressive towards me, and very jealous of my job, and he resented any attempt on my part to assist him. Healing can help every complaint, physical or mental, and knowing that he would not take it from me, I urged him to go to other healers I knew, but he refused.

He was prepared from time to time to see the family doctor, and it was not long before the doctor confirmed to me what I already knew. My husband was mentally sick.

# Chapter Seven

The doctor recommended that Richard should take up a completely different job, preferably one where he was his own boss. Easier said than done, but after due deliberation we came up with an idea. We would look for a small shop which Richard could run and which my daughter Margaret, who was now a young woman, could manage. Before long we bought a confectionery and fancy goods shop in Wanstead.

Although this change of occupation undoubtedly removed some pressure from Richard, I was surprised and disappointed that he did not seem interested in the shop. He was hardly ever there and left all the work to Margaret.

I came to the conclusion that Dick's problem was my success. The more I achieved in my job, the more he was diminished in his own eyes.

In a desperate attempt to save his sanity and our marriage, I decided we must work together as a partnership. I would literally sacrifice my job – a job I really loved – and he could give up the shop, which he seemed not to like. But what could we do together?

I had an idea, and I put it to him. My mother's people were hoteliers – my grandfather had owned the Spotted Dog in Barking and my brother John Maxwell had managed my uncle's pub the Britannia, also in Barking – and in fact my parents had met at a time when my widowed mother owned another East End public house. Why should we not buy a small hotel and run it together? We could sell both our house and the shop and use the proceeds towards the cost of the hotel.

Dick readily agreed, and I hoped that we might be starting out on a new and happier life together. Before very long we were the proud owners of the Wansfell Hotel in Chesswood Road, Worthing, with its twelve residents. It had no drinks licence, which suited me well because I had begun to suspect that Dick was a secret drinker.

It was mostly a residential hotel and did not cater for summer visitors. There were nine bedrooms on the upper floor. Downstairs were our own quarters, plus a huge kitchen and the residents' dining-room and lounge. There were two chalets with two fine outhouses in the garden which we kept for our family if they wanted to stay. This was 1964, and my son Brian was now aged twenty-four and already married; Margaret, aged nineteen, was sharing with a friend; my stepson Brian was married; and little Richard, the dwarf, was in South Africa with the Chipperfield Circus.

The place needed redecorating and modernizing, and this was one of the reasons I wanted it. My husband was very handy and I thought he would not only have a useful occupation but an important one. The hotel did indeed give him a new lease of life, at least for a time. He threw himself wholeheartedly into the work and within twelve months every room had been redecorated and the kitchen completely transformed. My doctor congratulated me on the cleanest kitchen she had ever seen.

We served three meals a day – breakfast, lunch and dinner – and we put kettles in every room so that our residents could make themselves tea. I do not think I ever worked harder in my life. I had an au pair and a cleaning woman, and sometimes Richard would help to serve the food, but I did all the marketing and all the cooking. I always cooked plenty, and there was no problem about second portions. All the food was home-made. I remember joking that it was no wonder I – meaning the hotel – was always full up; so were the guests!

It is not necessary to be stingy in order to make a profit. All that is necessary is good management. In any case I enjoyed running the hotel. I never regarded myself as off duty, although I did try to keep the evenings free. I only wished that Richard would involve himself with the same enthusiasm, but he soon lost interest.

The hotel became an enormous success. It was like a haven for elderly retired people, not unlike a healing home. One is not supposed to keep people in a hotel when they become ill, but I not only did so but actually looked after them. Indeed I gave guests healing when they requested it. They all knew about my work and about the Sunday-morning demonstrations of healing I gave in Brighton and Worthing – the only chance I had to practise my gift at that time, although even then I had always to be back to serve lunch at one o'clock.

One of my residents was a retired schoolteacher who kept herself very much to herself. She was very old and knew she was dying but did not want to go to hospital. She begged me to keep her in the hotel whatever happened, and in fact she died there at the age of ninety. She left me a hatbox which I still treasure. She was only one of many people who came to the hotel with one foot metaphorically in the grave who seemed to find a new lease of life. My doctor had a waiting list of people whenever I had a vacancy, but a vacancy only ever arose when someone died or a family moved away. At one time I had three blind people as residents, and I had to cut up all their food. I know I kept people whom most hotels would have refused, but I suppose I was not a typical hotelier.

Richard could have shared the success with me, but he chose to let me get on with things. I could never rely on him after our first year in the hotel. He made an effort if and when he wanted but the only job I was able to leave entirely to him (or so I thought) was the accounts.

61

I could not believe it on the first occasion when, without warning, he threw part of the guests' dinner, which he was supposed to be serving, on the floor. Something had upset him. When I questioned him, all he said was, 'Mind your own business.'

Of course it was unfortunately very much my business, and it became more so as his condition deteriorated. For no apparent reason – perhaps because he thought I had looked at him strangely or said something that displeased him – he would get terribly angry, even violent. On such occasions he might smash something. Twice he pulled the switchboard out of the wall – a serious inconvenience in a hotel – so that I could not ring the children or the doctor. There were times when I had to ring the police in self-protection. I was at my wits' end when I consulted the Medical Officer of Health, who of course came to the hotel as part of his duties; he said that there was nothing much he could do to help.

Richard was not always like this and I was sure that he loved me and the children and that he was not responsible for his violent actions when they occurred. Fortunately I am pretty tough and, although at times I was desperate, I thought probably I could cope with the problem if the outbursts were not too frequent. I became really alarmed however when one day he tried to hit me on the head with a hammer and succeeded in knocking out my front teeth.

I could even have put up with that had he not torn the blouse off the back of the au pair when she came to my aid. He rarely misbehaved in front of other people and was always charming to the guests and the staff, so this time I realized that something really had to be done. I telephoned my doctor, who came rushing over.

She found me in quite a state. Richard had by then calmed down and she had a long talk to him. 'We've got to have something done about you,' she told him, 'and I'm getting some doctors along.' In fact she returned later with the Medical Officer of Health and two other doctors. They first questioned me and then they spoke to Richard. I could hardly believe what he told them. I was going through the change of life, he said, and I had become mentally unbalanced. I had terrible fits of anger that I could not control and he needed protection!

I was staggered. Here was my husband attributing to me his own faults. I was not sure whether to feel sorry for him or for myself. The way he spoke, as much as what he said, distressed me. He handed round cigars to the medical men as if he had called them in on my account. Was there a suspicion of a hint that I, being psychic, was the unbalanced one? I even thought in my confusion that the doctors believed him, but as they left they told me that unless Richard wanted help, they could do nothing to get him into hospital.

Richard always apologized to me after his scenes, which proved to me that he knew what he was doing and that it was wrong.

I became worried when I found empty vodka bottles in the cellar and discovered that he had watered down the whisky in our drinks cupboard so that I would not notice that a quantity had disappeared. It was only then that I connected his violence with drinking. Later he was diagnosed as a manic depressive, his condition accelerated by alcohol. He was diagnosed independently also as a schizophrenic. Experts will understand what is meant by these descriptions. All I know is that his condition, whatever it was, did not make it easy for me to live with him.

I hate writing in these terms about a man I married, whom I loved and who loved me, particularly since he was the father of my stepchildren, but the reader will not think any the worse of my second husband because he was mentally ill. He could not have helped his behaviour, any more than if he had sneezed because he had a common cold.

I may have been at fault in deciding to break up the marriage, but there came a point at which I could not endure to live with Richard any longer. I did not think it was good for either of us to remain together. I agonized for days before I went to see a solicitor. He advised private treatment when I told him that there was no other reason for wanting to end the marriage than my husband's condition. Richard did eventually agree to see a psychiatrist in Brighton who recommended that he go into a nursing home as a patient. To my surprise, he agreed, but as soon as we were outside he turned on me and shouted, 'I'm going to kill you. You're trying to put me away.' There was a dreadful tension between us as I started to drive back to Worthing. Suddenly he wrenched the car wheel from me and tried to drive us over the edge into the sea. I fought him and somehow regained control of the car. He then lapsed into silence.

When we got home, I immediately telephoned the psychiatrist and told him what had happened. 'I can do nothing,' the man said, 'unless your husband comes in voluntarily.'

One week later Richard announced that he was going to London for the day. He did not say why, so I did not ask. I had long since given up questioning his movements. He left early and I got on with my work. Shortly after three in the afternoon he reappeared. His face was the colour of a beetroot and he looked quite strange. 'Tell that psychiatrist I'm going into the nursing home,' he said. He then told me that on the way up to town in the train he had felt very peculiar, and that on reaching London there were policemen turning every corner towards him wherever he walked.

To my great joy and relief, he went in for treatment the following day. It was shortly thereafter that the psychiatrist told me that Richard was insanely jealous of me and my work. He added however that Richard loved me dearly, and

I realized the truth of this when I received a letter from him in which he asked me to forgive him for his atrocious behaviour. He promised that he would never repeat it.

I was sadly too used to his apologies to lay much store by them, but I hoped that when he returned home after two months, things would be much better. But he was soon back to his old tricks, and this time he went to see his own doctor – not mine – and asked to be sent to a mental hospital for further treatment. He was away this time for six weeks and seemed much improved on his return. But then it started all over again . . .

I knew finally that my position was intolerable. I could not run the hotel and put up with Richard. If I were the sort of person to commit suicide – which I am not – I think I might well have taken my life at that time, so low and despondent did I feel. I had been happy in my first marriage for a long time; then it went sour. It was all happening again, like a replay of a tape, only louder and more strident. This was the nadir of my life.

After a truly dreadful day of scenes, I went to bed one night straight after dinner. It was too early to go to sleep and I sat up and thought about the awful events of the day and what to do to end the situation once and for all. I hated to admit failure. In any case, one divorce is enough in any woman's life. But I just could not go on.

I suddenly knew that my mother was with me in the room. I did not actually see her but I sensed her presence. This did not in any way surprise me because I have been fortunate at important times in my life to have received guidance not only from my parents but also from other spirit helpers. Then I heard her voice. It was loud and clear, and her message was unmistakable: 'You must be free,' she said. Then she told me that I should get a divorce. I thought to myself that that was easier said than done. As if reading my thoughts, my mother told me that if I sought a divorce immediately, I would get one very quickly.

I had the greatest respect for my mother's opinions but I did not regard her as the world's greatest legal expert. In those days it normally took a long time to obtain a divorce, and I did not particularly relish the prospect of a long-drawn-out process in which I would be airing my very dirty linen before other people. Perhaps if I put up with things, they would improve. I preached tolerance and understanding, so I should also practise them.

But instead of improving, matters got worse. I never knew from moment to moment when Richard would erupt. It was like walking a tightrope. My mother was right. I had to seek a divorce.

She was right even about the quick divorce. I think it was almost exactly six months after my mother came to me that I was granted a decree on the grounds of cruelty. I had already found a flat for Richard in Worthing, not too far from the hotel, where he went to live. He actually took a part-time job as a clerk with a motor firm. Later he returned to London where he got a job as a clerk in a hotel – the first of several such jobs.

I kept an eye on him, at least for the next four years until I met my present husband. On one occasion he asked me to remarry him, saying that he had learnt his lesson, and I actually took him back for three weeks, out of misplaced kindness, until I saw danger signals and sent him away again. My stepson Brian had the main responsibility of keeping watch on his father, and was very good to him right up to Richard's death in 1982.

Richard was of course a victim of his own nature, and he is a remarkable example of a man destroyed by an inability to adjust to new circumstances. After losing his job he was never the same man. On one occasion he had a blood test in hospital which revealed that the alcoholic content in his blood was quite incredibly higher than average. On being told this by the doctor who had taken the sample, Richard turned to the man and said, 'I never touch a drop.' This unhappy man lived in a world of make-believe. Unfortunately, other people had to inhabit that world alongside him.

I was so shaken by my second divorce that I felt I should seek a completely new life for myself. Although Richard had not been of much help in the hotel, and latterly a positive hindrance, at least I had had a man on the spot. Without him, I decided that running the hotel was too big a responsibility, much as I loved the work and my residents.

So one day, slightly older and a lot wiser, I sold the hotel, moved to a flat on the seafront and returned once more to my psychic work.

# Chapter Eight

oᏓooᏓooᏓo

The Spiritualist Association of Great Britain in London's Belgrave Square is the headquarters of the spiritualist movement in this country. When I sold the hotel I went to work there as a resident psychic from Monday to Friday. This entailed my living in London during the week and I returned to my flat in Worthing every Friday night for the weekend. I worked occasionally on the South Coast at the weekend, both as a psychic and as a healer.

I was one of eight or nine regular psychics at the Association at the time, and people who came along there for help were allocated to one or other of us according to our availability. Where possible they were sent to the psychic of their choice but very often they did not know a psychic by name or their particular choice might have been booked up, in which case they had either to see somebody else or make a forward appointment. I received a fee from the Association and did not personally charge the people who came to me. Additionally, I ran teaching classes at Belgrave Square, so I was never short of sitters and students.

I had my own way of operating and deliberately did not get too involved with the other psychics, although I had a very high respect for some of them. To use a modern phrase, I was too busy doing my own thing. God alone knows how many people I helped in my four years at the Association. People who were dissatisfied with their interviews were entitled to ask for their money back, but in only two cases during all that time did I have to admit failure. There were only two people I found I could not work with.

People keep coming up to me now at public meetings and

telling me how productive they found their interviews with me at Belgrave Square. What they do not always realize is that I probably do not remember them. All people are equally important to me at the time, and although many celebrities have crossed my path from all over the world – some even flying across the Atlantic specially to see me – I rarely recall what they said to me or what I said to them during a working interview. I have been astonished at times to read something in the press that I am supposed to have told some famous person. I never make notes or tape conversations or keep records, apart from an appointments diary, but I have no objection if my sitter wishes to do so.

If I remember examples of clairvoyance, it is usually because they have been repeated to me or been recorded in some way. Sometimes I remember the most important things; sometimes the most trivial – or what seem the most trivial, because it is not always what seems important that really is. One incident I shall never forget, for reasons that will be obvious, concerns Norah Blackwood, whom many people regarded as the top medium at the Association. I was dressing one morning, and since I was not taking a public meeting that day, I decided to put on a navy blue trouser suit, which was the sort of thing I often wore for consultations but which I would never have considered wearing if I were appearing before an audience on a platform. I suddenly had an image of Norah in my room. I did not see her physically. It was a mental image.

'Take that trouser suit off,' she said. I was rather put out by this strange request. 'You're not going to take my public meeting in a trouser suit,' she went on.

The image was so strong that I actually changed into a dress, feeling somewhat foolish, and it was in a dress that I arrived for work at Belgrave Square. Within half an hour there was a knock on my door. Minnie Bridges, another psychic, entered. 'Doris,' she said, 'Norah Blackwood's dead.'

'She's just spoken to me,' I managed to say. 'What's happened?'

'We really don't know,' Minnie replied, 'but we've just heard she passed away last night.' So she was already dead when she told me to change my clothes! I went downstairs and when I was given my schedule for the day, my name was there to take Norah's public meeting.

Taking any sort of meeting at short notice was by then second nature to me. I did not even have to prepare myself. I was even dressed for the occasion. But my mind went back some years to my very first public meeting. How I had changed in the meantime and grown both in confidence and in experience.

Ever since I first took an interest in spiritualism, I had been involved in the movement as an individual, and I had become a healer also, but I had never thought of myself as a public psychic or a public healer because I did not want to accept the responsibility. Young psychics do not always realize that a person's whole life can be affected by what a psychic tells him. One has therefore to be very careful, very precise, in the advice one gives. I felt able to advise privately, but not in public.

There had been several occasions when I had been asked to take the platform and stand in for a psychic who for some reason had failed to arrive, but I had always refused. One day, shortly after my second marriage, I was in the chair at a public meeting, and it was my job to introduce the excellent medium who was taking the meeting. All started normally and he had communications for two people in the audience. However, instead of continuing, he startled me by saying, 'Now I'm told by those who use me that I must sit down, and Doris Collins is going to take over.'

70

This was the very challenge I had always refused to accept, and I was absolutely petrified. I stood up and my legs felt as though they were giving way under me. I opened my mouth but no words came. I tried to concentrate, but I saw and heard nothing. No spirit guide came to my rescue, and I had no message for anyone in the audience.

I thought to myself that this was the end of my 'career' as a psychic, public or otherwise. After this fiasco my reputation would be worthless. What on earth could I do?

All at once I had the slightly wicked idea to invent messages, to let my imagination run riot, and before I knew what I was doing, I heard myself spouting the most incredible rubbish – or so I thought – naming names and stating dates as I made up stories. I was quite astonished that I appeared to be getting away with it, and when the meeting was over people came up to me and told me how impressed they were, how what I had told them had been correct, and so on. I thought what gullible fools they were, and as they continued to congratulate me I confessed that I had invented it all.

They obviously did not believe me. They laughed, no doubt thinking I was joking. I later learnt that I had told the Secretary of the church where the meeting had taken place that he and his wife would on a particular date move house and buy a shop. He worked as a first-aid man in a factory and was very surprised at my message, but in fact what I thought I had invented actually occurred, on the exact date. There were similar examples of my nonsense proving true, but I did not know this at the time. I hardly slept for a week, so disturbed was I by my deception. I was also worried that, although I had clairvoyant powers which I had used successfully in the past, when it came to using them in public my mind had been a blank.

It was only later that I was told that the speaker I had introduced had been informed by those who used him that I

71

was to begin public work. He had therefore dropped me in at the deep end, and amazingly I had impressed a number of spiritualist church leaders in the audience who now begged me to accept engagements in their churches. I felt this was not possible. It would not have been honest of me, but they were so insistent that, despite my protests, I was persuaded to take a single public meeting at Woodford Spiritualist Church, where I was on home ground. I prayed that my genuine clairvoyant gifts would operate for me this time.

I was nervous as a kitten as the day approached for my first public meeting on my own as a clairvoyant. I wondered if my mind would go blank again. I was determined not to let my imagination run riot if all else failed. On the day, I sat by myself in a little room adjacent to the main hall, and closed my eyes in prayer. The hall was beginning to fill and I felt rather agitated. Then I looked up and saw my father. He was standing in front of me, quite clearly, and he lectured me gently:

'What are you worried about?' he asked. 'The only way to deal with you was to throw you in and make you swim. Now go out and work. You're not on your own. You'll get all the help you need if you ask for it. And as your life goes on, you'll need much more courage in future than you need today. The trouble with you is that you've always been too independent. You don't do this work alone. Many people are there to help you if you ask them.'

Immediately I felt elated. I knew I was not going to fail. Everybody said that my first public meeting was a success, and I have not looked back since. Years later I was twice to take meetings at the Royal Albert Hall for the spiritualists' annual remembrance service. In between, by the time I was asked to replace Norah Blackwood at very short notice, conducting a meeting was second nature to me.

Following Norah's death, my workload at the Association

72

increased even more and I was often booked up a long time ahead. As one would expect at Belgrave Square, the main psychic centre in the country, the mediums who worked there were all very talented, although they varied in their degree of experience. I hope it will not be regarded as a criticism of one of them if I tell the following story about him; it is not intended as such. He was giving a sitting to a lady during the course of which there were three loud knocks, which at first he ignored. When they were repeated, he said, 'That must be somebody trying to make their presence felt. Come in, friend.' Whereupon a skylight opened and in came a workman who had been trapped on the roof and had been signalling that he was having trouble getting back in!

There was one particular event that happened at about that time which I have reason to remember. During one of my teaching classes, a woman member of our group was contacted, through me, by a man who told her that he had been killed by his wife, and he thanked the woman for looking after his children.

This was an unusual message even for someone as experienced as I was in receiving messages, but it made complete sense to our woman member. Her husband was a doctor who had attended a family where the wife had been tried for murder following her husband's death. According to the trial records, the husband had come home one night, having been drinking, and a terrific row ensued during which the wife took hold of her husband's tie and pulled it tight. He rolled back on the bed in what the wife thought was a drunken stupor, but in fact he had been strangled. The wife was acquitted of murder but convicted and imprisoned for manslaughter, and the doctor and his wife, who was one of my sitters, had taken care of the children, two sons aged seventeen and sixteen at the time.

What I did not realize then is that my sitter's husband,

73

the doctor, had previously consulted me privately. I could not have known this because the lady did not use her married name. He had subsequently confirmed that I told him that I had a message for him from a man who had recently passed over in a tragic manner. The man expressed his gratitude to my sitter and his wife for what they were doing for his family, and he also said that he was very sorry for what had happened and that nobody was to blame.

There was no way I could have connected the two messages, one to the husband and one to the wife, using a different surname, even if I had remembered the first message at the time I received the second. What is even stranger is that over a year later the husband sent his eighteen-year-old son to see me under an assumed name so that I could not possibly have connected the boy with either of his parents. Apparently the message was repeated through me for the third time. I am indebted to the doctor, the boy's father, for this information that confirms something I would not otherwise have known, namely that I passed on similar messages from the same person to three different people on three different occasions.

Of course I never know at the time whether the messages I receive and relay are important or trivial. A message from a man who has been strangled accidentally by his wife may be more significant than a message about a pair of kippers, but who knows? It is a matter for the recipient, and often a seemingly unimportant communication may have the greatest significance.

I do not know why the kipper story stays in my mind. Perhaps because it was reported in the press. It happened in 1972, two years after I first received a message from the man who had been strangled. I had been engaged to take the annual reunion service of the Greater World Church Association. There was a big meeting in a packed Friends House in Euston Road. I worked for over an hour and at

74

one point a lady came to me from the spirit world who indicated that she wanted to contact her husband. I have often been asked how I find a particular person in an audience. I cannot give what most people would regard as a satisfactory answer. I just somehow know where the person is. I 'go' to him. This does not mean that I physically leave the platform – although I could if I wish, of course – but that I point to where the person is.

On this occasion, because the lady told me or because I sensed it, or for whatever other reason, I knew her husband was in the gallery. I sense, I see, I feel, I hear, I know – and beyond that I cannot explain.

The lady told me that her husband was a chef. He had been trained at the Savoy and he could cook the most rich and rare dishes, but his own greatest treat, which she always prepared for him when he came home to tea on Saturday, was a pair of kippers. I found the man in the audience. 'I see you having kippers,' I told him. 'It's your wife, presenting a plate of kippers as some sort of evidence.' The man, who had become a spiritualist, did not in fact need evidence that it really was his wife who wanted to speak to him, but he later told me that if ever he had needed proof, I could not have found better evidence than the kippers. There is a footnote to this fishy story. A few days later at another meeting I saw the same man in the audience, once again in the gallery. Something made me call out to him. 'It's not kippers this time, it's herrings,' I said, and I told the gathering about our previous encounter. I told them that the man was a great chef but that he liked to go home to a pair of kippers, but that on that day he was going home to herrings. This happened to be true, as the man confirmed, and for some reason everyone was in fits of laughter. I am not a funny person and I do not easily tell jokes but one would have thought I was the star attraction at the Palladium.

75

Spiritualism is not a laughing matter but there is no reason why it should always be approached with deadly seriousness. Its purpose is to help, and there are many different ways of providing help. There are also different methods of communication between the spirit and the physical worlds. Hence there are differences in the way in which mediums operate.

I am often asked whether women make better mediums than men do. I do not think so. Quality has nothing to do with sex. It is possible that, because a psychic is a sensitive and sensitivity tends perhaps to be more a feminine than a masculine attribute, women make better psychics, but I am not sure that that is true. There are many very good male psychics, but more women seem to practise. This may be due to no more significant a reason than that most male psychics are in full-time employment whereas many women psychics are housewives who can work psychically on a part-time basis if they have the time.

In my teaching classes, I usually had as many male as female students. I always made a point of interviewing each new applicant. There was no virtue in someone coming to study with me unless I felt that he or she had some psychic potential that I could mould. I usually had about a dozen students at each session in Belgrave Square.

One of the applicants was a man called Philip McCaffrey. He disturbed me for some reason. I felt he was going to be a nuisance in my class. 'I don't think I'm the right person for you to study under,' I told him.

'Why?' he asked.

'I have no reason, except I think you should have a man to teach you,' I said somewhat lamely. I felt he was pushy.

'I've watched you work,' he responded, 'and I want to study under you.'

'I'll think about it,' I said. 'I'll carry on with my interviewing if you'll wait outside the door.'

This was a rather cheeky thing for me to say to a distinguished insurance broker, a former naval officer, in his late forties. He was in fact only eight years younger than I was, and here I was treating him like some teenager. He told me later that he almost walked out but that something stopped him. For my part, I regarded him as sincere. He had told me that he had studied comparative religion and that he had become interested in both psychic and healing work because he believed that he had gifts in that direction. I agreed finally to accept him, and he thanked me.

For several weeks he made my class difficult by asking questions to which I thought he knew the answers. I could only think that he was trying to score over me in some way. Other students asked me why I put up with him, and I replied that I was sure he was potentially very psychic.

As it happened, this particular class progressed excellently, and Philip along with it. He gradually became more aware and we were very much in tune. More than one student from that class who started with me now works as a psychic on the public platform.

One of my students was a customs officer whose mother I knew well, and each Friday night he used to take me out to dinner before I returned for the weekend to Worthing. One Friday night, Philip came to me and said, 'I've told Julian. I'm taking you to dinner tonight.'

'Who said so?' I demanded.

'I've made all arrangements,' was his reply, as if that were final.

I was so taken aback that I agreed. 'Where are we going?' I asked.

'I'm not telling you,' he said. It turned out to be a lovely restaurant in Richmond with a Latin-American guitarist.

During dinner, without warning, Philip suddenly said, 'I'm going to marry you.'

The proverbial feather would have a job at the best of

times in knocking down someone as solid as I am, but I confess that I was quite astounded. Twice bitten, I thought, thrice shy. 'You must be out of your mind,' I said ungraciously. 'I'm not marrying anybody.'

'Oh, yes, you will,' he said with supreme confidence. 'I've known it for a long time.'

After dinner Philip drove me to the station and saw me onto the Worthing train. Thereafter we dined together at least once a week, and I became more and more interested in him as I got to know him. Then one day in his flat in Kensington he wanted to measure my finger to see what size ring I wore. I was quite bowled over when he asked me what kind of ring I would like.

I protested that, having made two bad marriages, I dared not risk a third. Philip, like Jack, had never been married before; but I had had more than my fair share of marriage. 'I'm not an easy person to live with,' I said, trying to dissuade him, 'because I have to be free.'

His reply interested me. 'I've studied you very closely,' he told me, 'for over two years, and I know the only way to keep you is to give you room to breathe. I won't tie you up.'

The fact that Philip was slightly younger than I was did not worry me. I was more concerned that he was a Catholic and I was not. As a child, I had had a traumatic experience following an attack of peritonitis which kept me in hospital for six weeks. I was sent to convalesce in Folkestone in a home run by nuns. In every corridor there seemed to be a carving of Jesus on the cross, a crown of thorns on his head and blood running down his hands and feet. This upset me terribly and I felt that my own hands had nails through them. On Sundays I sneezed when the incense was swung. The nuns glided about silently on the highly polished wooden floors, and there was a mysterious atmosphere about the place. I felt shut in as if I were in prison.

Of course this was a lot of nonsense, but to an impressionable eight-year-old it was an unpleasant experience, and I did everything I knew to escape from the nuns. I suppose it must have coloured my thinking in later life because although all people are alike to me whatever their religion, I hesitated about marrying a Catholic – until Philip told me that his two sisters had married Jews, after which I felt much better!

There was also the problem that I was about to make an important professional visit to the United States and Mexico, and this really was therefore a ridiculous time to embark again on marriage, but Philip would not take no for an answer. Finally I suggested we get engaged. 'We can think about marriage later,' I said. Philip agreed at once and asked me what sort of engagement ring I wanted. As I had chosen my last two rings, I decided I might have better luck if I left the choice this time to him.

We became engaged in March 1973, shortly before my first major exposure in the United States. I suddenly realized how stupid it was at our age to be engaged and not married. I just felt I had to marry Philip, having gone so far, and on an impulse I told him so. He reacted as though he had expected me to say so, and rushed off to get a special licence. We were married on 30 March, four days before I was due to fly to America. Only our close family knew, and we decided to keep the marriage a secret for the time being, at least until after the American tour.

One of the people we had to tell was my old friend Peter Sellers, who had been to me many times for private consultations. He had flown back from Italy (where he was filming) to be my guest of honour at the annual dinner and dance of the mediums' union, of which I was Vice-President. At the dinner Peter stood up and made an amusing speech, delighting the audience. I was not so delighted however when he announced to all the world that Philip and I were husband and wife.

Our secret was a secret no longer and the gathering, in a London hotel, turned into a riotous celebration party. Peter joined the band and played the drums all night until we broke up.

So little Doris Cooper who became Doris Lawless and then Doris Collins (by which name she is still known professionally), was now Mrs Philip McCaffrey.

# Chapter Nine

o◯oo◯oo◯o

I had already spent three months in America during the second half of 1972, and an extraordinary three months they were. I returned again early in 1973, straight after my marriage to Philip. On the second occasion at least I had some idea of what I was letting myself in for.

Psychic work and healing are the same all over the world, but they are more so in the United States. If that sounds ridiculous, what I mean is that everything in America is done on a vast scale and at breakneck pace. I think that in the short time I spent there at that period of my life I became more of a celebrity than I had become in over thirty years working at home. Indeed the pressures on me, and the financial inducements made to me, to uproot myself and make my home permanently in America were so persuasive that I actually gave serious thought to the possibility before finally deciding to remarry and remain at home. I had so many well-paid offers to stay in the States, including one of a job as resident healer at a clinic that two doctors were setting up in California, but I preferred the British way of life to which I was accustomed.

It was made clear to me however that I could always return, and as often as I liked. There would be plenty I could do whenever I had the time to travel across the Atlantic, and I have in fact been back many times. I now have many good friends in America and it is always a pleasure to visit them.

The essential difference between British and American psychics is that we are trained to prove survival, whereas many Americans are trained to predict the future. I often predict things in the ordinary course of my work, but I hesitate to predict in the deliberate way that they do. I am more concerned with people's personal lives than with world events. The one and only time I ever predicted an event publicly was towards the end of 1976, and I was more or less forced into it. I was asked to take part in a radio programme as a member of a panel. Our subject was the year ahead and the recorded discussion was to be transmitted on New Year's Day. We talked about current events in the world and, without warning, the chairman of the panel asked me what I predicted for 1977.

Although this was something I would not normally have done, I felt obliged to co-operate, at least to the extent of considering the question. I remember shutting my eyes and concentrating, and suddenly I was aware of a disastrous air crash. I saw an aeroplane and felt an explosion. I was aware of terrible carnage.

I do not believe in telling people that they are going to die or be involved in tragedy. I aim to comfort and not to alarm. I may warn somebody off a particular course of action if I believe it to be potentially harmful, but that is an entirely different matter. On this occasion I was dealing impersonally with an event that I knew would happen, but I did not know where or in what circumstances. I therefore recorded exactly what I had seen, and the programme was broadcast in several countries. The prediction is therefore on record.

Early in 1977 I was boarding an aircraft to fly back to England from Florida. I was chatting to a fellow traveller and I asked her if she knew how long we would be stopping in New York on the way back. 'This is a through flight to England,' she said. I looked at my ticket – how could I have forgotten? – and of course it was a direct flight. I must have made a mistake, and yet I had a strong feeling that I was right. Alan Whicker was on the same plane and I remember talking to him.

At one point I went to the toilet to freshen up and, while there, I saw a bright flash and I heard a bang. This instantly brought to mind my prediction about an air disaster, and for one awful moment I thought that I had foreseen a ghastly event in which I myself was a participant. Had I actually foretold my own death?

I returned to my seat as quickly as possible, and everything seemed normal. Nobody appeared bothered. I sat very calm and said nothing. I knew however with absolute certainty that the prediction I had made would come true.

I had not in fact been imagining things, because the captain's voice came over the loudspeaker. 'Ladies and gentlemen,' he said, 'there is no cause for alarm but we have to turn back to New York. We can't continue over the Atlantic . . .' Apparently we had lost two engines!

So I had been right about stopping over in New York, and I had also seen an actual flash and heard an actual bang. But the accident I had foreseen was not to that particular flight. I knew however that it would not be long delayed. Almost exactly a week later there was a terrible disaster in Tenerife. I had long forgotten the details of what I had foretold when the chairman of our panel telephoned me to say how accurately I had predicted exactly what in fact had occurred.

But, as I have said, I prefer to leave the prediction of future events to others. Americans may be more curious about the future than we are, and perhaps that is why American psychics so readily oblige them with predictions. But that does not mean American psychics are in any way inferior to British. The psychic gift knows no nationality; it crosses all frontiers.

I had originally been invited to America by Dr Charles Pons, an optometrist from Glendale, California. He had had a sitting with me in London and must have been impressed because he not only asked me to stay with him but offered to sponsor me. He had become interested in psychic phenomena after visiting the Philippines to see the so-called psychic surgeons, the most famous of whom was Tony Agpaoa. I shall have something to say about these remarkable people later, when I tell the story of my own visit to them. They had apparently cured Dr Pons's diabetes.

I was one of many mediums and healers whom Dr Pons saw while in England, and he told his American friends that I was the 'greatest'. No doubt he was exaggerating, but his recommendation did no harm to my reputation. He introduced me to Lee Atkinson. She and her husband were entrepreneurs for psychics and she made contacts for me to appear on radio and television in many different parts of the States.

For some reason I was a sensation. I had never experienced the sort of success and the amount of publicity I was achieving. My audiences were bowled over by what I said, and on one occasion the studio switchboard could not cope with the flood of telephone calls that were coming in to me. I decided to work normally and to take it in my stride.

It is easier for me to remember what happened in America because so much of it was recorded in one way or another. Hilly Rose, for example, wrote a book in 1978 in which he mentioned me. He had a radio show in Los Angeles, and I was introduced to him by Lee Atkinson. Both in his book and in the press accounts were given of some of the things I did and said which so impressed people, but they do not seem to me to be particularly worthy of repetition. What is interesting is that the following year I again appeared on his programme, but this time without leaving England.

I broadcast from Romford to California by Telstar. The programme was beamed from coast to coast to an audience estimated at a quarter of a million people. Unfortunately I could not hear any of the people who telephoned the radio station with questions for me, and every question and answer had to be relayed through Hilly Rose in person. What at first seemed a disaster in fact turned out to be a blessing in disguise because even the sceptics who thought that I achieved my results by some sort of mind reading could not believe that I could read people's minds whom I could not even hear, let alone see, at a distance of six thousand miles.

The programme lasted an hour, with only a five-minute break. The response was overwhelming. Apparently I hit the bull's eye, so to speak, time and time again, and my accuracy caused a sensation. In his book Hilly Rose explains how he investigated psychics on his programme for two years. He says that he was beginning to be bored with them when he was introduced to me. 'Some were funny, some weird,' he wrote, and 'just one was so incredibly accurate she could almost make a believer out of an agnostic.' This was a very handsome tribute to me, for which I am humbly grateful. Perhaps he was impressed by what I told him about himself. He had a young girl working for him and I told him on the radio that he would marry her. He scoffed at the idea at the time, but it was not all that long afterwards that he sent me a return air ticket to their wedding in San Francisco.

I had always known that clairvoyance worked at a distance, but even I was surprised at my apparent achievement on the Hilly Rose show. The attractive virtue of the Americans is that they are not afraid to experiment. It was brave of Hilly to gamble on my being able to function successfully across the ocean, but he was prepared to try. Other people gave me the opportunity to heal on radio and television. It is only comparatively recently that the phone-in programme has become a feature of British broadcasting. In America I would appear, for example, on a radio

85

show and people with ailments would telephone me to see if I could help them. 'Hello, Doris,' they usually began, and I immediately identified their problem. 'Oh, you've got a bad back,' I might have said. 'How on earth did you know?' was the almost invariable answer. It would have taken too long to explain and I never did. Instead I placed my hands, mentally of course, on the affected part. Many callers told me that they suddenly felt heat in a part of their body, and their pains very often disappeared almost immediately. Strange as this may seem to people who have not experienced absent healing, there is in America plenty of recorded evidence about my results in this field.

One of the people I was asked to heal – though not at a distance – was Sidney Omar, the famous astrologer. His ex-wife, Jeraldine Saunders, had heard me on the radio and begged me to see Sidney, who was ill. She collected me and drove me to Santa Monica. Her former husband was a household name in America. I knew little about astrology and have never functioned as a fortune-teller, but I have always kept an open mind about things I do not understand, and I knew that Mr Omar was highly respected among people who claimed to understand astrology.

As I walked into the room where he was sitting, he pointed at me and said, 'Give me a number.' He was obviously interested in numerology, having written a book on the subject. I mentioned the first number that came into my head – I forget what it was – and he assured me that I had chosen a 'master' number, which meant that I was all right. I felt very relieved, and I proceeded to give him healing for what was wrong with him. He then asked if I would give him a sitting, and I found myself telling him a number of very personal things. Obviously they were of a confidential nature and although I happen to remember certain things I said, I cannot repeat them. One matter only I feel sure Sidney would not object to my divulging: Sidney

Omar, the name by which he was known professionally, was not in fact his real name, and I think he was quite astonished when I revealed his actual name to him during the sitting – a name known to hardly anyone outside his close family.

We later became firm friends, and he was one of the many people who tried to persuade me to remain in America. I made a prediction about his ex-wife Jeraldine, who remained such a good friend to him even after their divorce. She was a cruise director, and I forecast that she would write something that would become successful throughout the world. She laughed at me disbelievingly, but if anybody remembers *The Love Boat* and will take the trouble to discover who wrote it, they will find that her name was Jeraldine Saunders.

There are two other stories I should like to relate about America, and they both started with what appeared to me to be exceptional rudeness. In Britain, even those uninformed people who regard spiritualism as mumbo-jumbo and mediums as charlatans are unlikely to tell me to my face that I am a phoney. But in America, where by and large people are very kind and polite to a visiting Englishwoman, I had two such impolite confrontations.

My first visit to New York was in the company of two other British psychics, Kathleen St George and Coral Polge, the psychic artist, and the renowned healer Tom Johanson, who is Coral's husband. Coral and I often worked together in front of an audience. She would draw portraits of people from the spirit world and I would connect them with people in the audience.

We were working together before an audience at Hunter College. In between sessions I was resting in my room, and I asked not to be disturbed because the work was exhausting and I badly needed to recharge my batteries. I was disturbed however by the telephone. It was the lady who was organizing our arrangements, and in a slightly awed voice she said, 'Mr Alan Burke is here and he wants to see you.' I told her that I absolutely had to rest and could see nobody. Ten minutes later the phone rang again. Mr Burke, it appeared, would not take no for an answer, but I was very emphatic about not seeing him or anyone else because I needed that quiet hour. I closed my eyes and drifted off, not thinking who this Mr Burke was and why he had to see me so urgently.

I was awoken by a knock on the door. I opened the door in my dressing gown to be confronted by four men. I was unusually angry. 'Who are you and what do you want?' I demanded.

'I'm Alan Burke,' one of the men said, 'and I've come to prove you're a fraud.'

Before I could react, all four men were in my room and I realized that three of them were a camera crew.

I rushed into the bathroom to dress. I did not know at the time that Mr Burke had from time to time tried to expose psychics on his television programme and that many people walked in fear of him. He certainly had me at a disadvantage.

'I've seen you operate,' he said, 'and I don't believe in what you do.' He obviously, it seemed to me, traded on his rudeness.

I do not think I have ever been so angry in my life, but I decided that the best way to deal with him was not to respond in kind but instead to prove to him that I was genuine. Instinctively I let the clairvoyance flow, and as I did so I heard the cameras begin to roll. I told him so much about himself and his family that he was quite flabbergasted, and he told me that he was completely satisfied about my honesty. He actually offered to fly me over weekly from England to take part in his show, and he confirmed this offer on television in his next programme when he said that he regarded many psychics as 'kooks' but that I was the only one he had ever met who was completely genuine.

I thought at first he was one of the rudest men I had ever met, but I realize now that I misjudged him initially despite his unfortunate way of putting my back up. Perhaps he thought that I would not respond so well unless he created an antagonistic situation. At all events, he and I became close friends and some time later he introduced me to his former wife. I told him that they would remarry. I could see that he did not believe me, but I was right. About three years ago I received a telegram from him informing me about the wedding. 'Love is better the second time around,' he wrote.

If he was rude, what was I to think of the reporter who came to interview me for the *National Enquirer*? He had made no appointment – as he told me later, so that I could not check up on him – and his opening words were: 'I don't believe a word of what you're going to tell me.'

I asked him why in that case he had bothered to come. He said he had got to write about me because he had been sent by his editor. His name was Hal Jacques. He was a hard-bitten journalist who had covered literally thousands of stories in his time. He is now a very dear friend, and I am indebted to him for details of some of the things that I told him which he reported in his newspaper and later confirmed to me in a letter.

I did not in fact tell him anything very different from what I told other people, but he is one of the few persons who actually recorded what I said at the time. To that extent his evidence will be interesting to those who want to know the sort of things that I am often impelled to say.

Hal was not a sitter in the normal sense. He had not come to me for a consultation about himself; he had come to investigate me. It seems however that after about twenty minutes of normal discussion, I suddenly held up my hand.

'I must interrupt,' I said, according to him. 'I hadn't intended giving you a reading but I am being given a message which concerns you. Would you care to hear it?'

He leaned forward with interest. 'I am being told about a house in London,' I said. 'I am being shown a workshop where people are engaged in tailoring. They are sewing buttonholes in men's waistcoats. Does that mean anything to you?'

It did indeed. Hal was only six years old when his parents emigrated from London to New York, and I was reminding him over fifty years later of the basement workshop in the East End where his grandparents had lived and where the children did simple tailoring work. Not surprisingly perhaps, the sceptical reporter who had not been over-impressed in his previous encounters with psychics was now listening to me intently.

I am always being given names, and the names Sarah and Leah came to me strongly. Hal's maternal grand-mother was called Sarah, but he knew no one called Leah. It was days later that he asked his aunt about Leah. 'Don't you know?' the woman said. 'Leah was Grandma's middle name. Her name was Sarah Leah.' Only then did Hal remember that as a child he had called his grandmother by her Jewish name Soorahlaya. He had always believed that it meant little Sarah. In fact Soorah was Sarah and Laya was Leah, and he had never realized this until I had unlocked the door to his memory of his grandmother.

The many other things I told him do not seem to me to be of very great interest but they were enough to cause him to describe me as the most accurate medium-psychic he had ever encountered. But he would only give me 99 out of 100 for accuracy because I had mentioned one name that he knew was wrong. Even his aunt could identify no one in the family who had died called Sam. The only Sam was his uncle, who was alive and well in Canada – or so he thought

90

until a cousin in Toronto telephoned to say that Uncle Sam had died some time ago. Thereafter I could do no wrong in the eyes of my sceptical reporter.

He did as much as anybody to tell the American people about me.

# Chapter Ten

o⊖oo⊖oo⊖o

I am now a seasoned traveller, and my name is known to people in many parts of the world. One journey I shall never forget was my first visit to Australia in 1974.

The very mention of Australia had always had a romantic connotation for me. I remember my father telling me that his father – my grandfather – had gone there as a young man and disappeared. After about ten years my great-grandfather had inserted advertisements in Australian newspapers, as a result of which my grandfather's passage had been paid back to England. My father had been very impressed that his father had, so he said, attended the first Test Match in Australia between the two countries.

There was another Australian connection – my brother Fred. He had emigrated when I was a young child, and it was while I was still running the hotel that the idea came to me to try to track him down, but I did nothing about it at the time.

Of my father's children, George was dead – as of course was Emmie – and Johnny had long since vanished from my world. There was only Fred about whom I felt strongly. I had always had a soft spot for him, as I believe he had for me. All three of my mother's sons – Will, John and Stuart – were dead, and I had lost touch with Lily. Fred was closest to me of all my brothers. He used to take me to music lessons, and for walks, when he was home on leave from the Merchant Navy, and what I loved about him was that he never criticized me or my actions; he understood me better than the others did.

I knew that he had jumped ship in Australia at the age of twenty-one or twenty-two, and had never returned home in all the intervening years. He would now be in his sixties. Mother used to read me his letters, but since her death I had hardly heard of him. All I knew was that he had written from Brisbane, but I had no address for him and in any case he would probably have moved in the meantime.

Yet I kept thinking about him, and there was this nagging feeling that I must see him. I seemed to remember that he had ridden on a ranch, and that he had bought a farm which he had lost through drought or famine – but whether this was reality or childish fantasy, I did not know. One of his last letters to my mother – his stepmother – told us that he was married and had a child.

Then one day I heard my father's voice telling me that I would be going to Australia to see Fred. Not long afterwards I was looking through some old snapshots when out fell a letter that Fred had written to Mother over thirty years previously. I had looked at these same photographs several times before without ever finding the letter. It had Fred's old address in Brisbane.

I took a chance and wrote to him there, marking the envelope 'Please forward'. A reply came within a fortnight. Fred still lived in the same house but he wrote from the hospital where he was recovering from a serious coronary. 'Your letter nearly gave me another one,' he said and told me how thrilled he was to hear from me.

In my next letter I asked whether he ever thought of coming home for a visit because I so much wanted to see him, and he replied that his health was such that he did not think he could make the journey now. He had had his own business for many years but had retired because of his condition. He told me that his daughter Cheryl, who was now a social worker, had been in England for a couple of years on a working holiday and had tried unsuccessfully to trace me. She was however planning to return for a holiday with two other girls, and she would definitely look me up.

In fact all three girls came to stay with me at the hotel, and Cheryl told me how much her father wanted to see me. I took them all to a meeting in Brighton at which I was working. Cheryl was very impressed apparently and wrote and told her father. His next letter was interesting. 'It's strange, Doris,' he wrote. 'I always knew, even when you were a little girl, there was something quite different about you. I fully believe what you do because I've had similar experiences. My wife and I went to Tasmania on a holiday and we visited an old prison. I had a strange feeling I'd been there before and I could even take my wife to where the kitchens had been and describe the whole place.'

I was ready for any excuse to see my brother Fred, but I had problems in my life that made it difficult for me to do so. It was not until after my marriage to Philip that I started to think about it again. Philip is a very kind man, and one day he said to me: 'Doris, if it's your heart's wish, go.'

This was all the encouragement I needed and I started to make plans. I mentioned these to Maurice Barbanell, who was then editor of *Psychic News*, and he said he hoped I would do some work in Australia and not just go for the sake of Fred. 'They need psychic workers very badly,' he said, and suggested I write to Don Davis. Don was President of the Spiritual Healers' Association of Australia, and in response to my question whether there was anything I could do in Australia for a week or two, he replied, 'My God, is there?'

My intended flying visit turned out to be something altogether different – a three-month absence in which I went also to the Philippines and to New Zealand. When I told Marjorie Horton about going to Australia, she told me that she had a brother in New Zealand and suggested that

94

she come with me to Australia and then fly on to see her brother, leaving me behind. Marjorie, a retired hospital matron, was a good friend, and I leapt at the idea. It was she who put it in my mind to go to New Zealand myself after visiting Australia.

It was while discussing this with Philip that I brought up the notion of taking in the Philippines en route. As a spiritual healer I very much wanted to see the psychic healers in the Philippines about whom I had heard so much, and this seemed too good an opportunity to miss.

Philip, bless him, fell in with my ambitious plans, although he could not accompany me for business reasons. I think he was pleased that Marjorie would travel with me at least part of the way. Thus began a long and exhausting tour that had never a dull moment for me, nor I hope for the audiences in Australia and New Zealand who made just as big a fuss of me as had the Americans.

We went first to the Philippines, where our arrival was far from auspicious. We had to change planes in Hong Kong and wait for a long time at the airport. I suddenly had a strange feeling about my luggage which gradually became an absolute conviction: something would go wrong in the transfer from BOAC to Qantas. So strong was my feeling that I actually asked to be shown the suitcases, but I was told that this was impossible and that nothing ever went wrong.

Sure enough when we arrived in Manila at 11 p.m., there was no luggage. I had nothing except the clothes I was wearing, not even a toothbrush, and Marjorie's clothes could never have fitted me. It was stiflingly hot even at that time of night and I was almost literally torn between the airline official who was filling out the necessary forms and the taxi driver who had been ordered to meet us.

'Please come, please come,' the driver was tugging at my one and only dress, 'I must take you to hotel.'

95

'I can't go until I've got my luggage sorted out,' I tried to explain. The airline were preparing some sort of chit that would authorize me to make certain essential purchases the following day until my missing luggage turned up.

'Come now,' the driver insisted. 'Martial law.'

'Martial law?' I enquired. 'What's that got to do with me?'

'Curfew,' was the reply. 'Twelve o'clock. Nobody must be in streets after midnight. Otherwise prison.'

I knew all about Cinderella, but this was ridiculous. There was more tugging and the driver announced that the penalty for breaking the curfew was not only prison overnight but: 'Tomorrow we all sweep the streets.'

I am normally a very calm person but I was coming near to anger. It is only in retrospect that I see the funny side of it. Eventually I got my piece of paper from the airline and the taxi driver deposited us at our hotel as the clock struck twelve. He was in such a hurry to depart that he did not even wait for a tip.

Our hotel was in the main street opposite the American Embassy and we had one of the best rooms overlooking the street. The first thing I did was rinse out my underclothes and hang them out to dry for the next day.

In the morning, armed with the authority from the airline, I went shopping for clothes. I had gone to bed in my slip. Everywhere I went I was greeted politely: the assistants placed their hands together, bowed and then went into fits of giggles. They spoke to each other in their own language, which unfortunately I did not understand – but what was clear was that they could not, or would not, help me. It was almost a ritual, and after three shops I began to think I was among the most peculiar people I had ever encountered.

In the fourth shop I struck lucky. At least I met an assistant who spoke English. I told him I wanted a dress and some underclothes, and he too started to giggle.

'What's the matter?' I demanded. 'Why does everyone laugh?'

'Well, lady,' he said, 'we are very little people and you are very big lady. Staff too polite to tell you.'

He suggested that they make me 'a very fine shirt'. I explained that I also needed something to go underneath. 'We can make it very long,' he replied, helpfully.

In fact a day before we left Manila, a beautiful shirt was delivered to the hotel in cream-coloured linen, magnificently embroidered down the front. The trouble was that it came down below my knees. It would have fitted an elephant, and large as I am, I am not quite that size. I could just imagine myself conducting a meeting in Sydney in that get-up.

So despite the great heat, I wore the same clothes more or less every day.

That was not my only problem. On our fourth day in Manila, crowds began to assemble in the street outside the hotel at seven o'clock in the morning. The heat was intense, and around midday Marjorie and I were resting on top of our beds when there was a sharp knock on the door and the manager entered, accompanied by two soldiers with machine-guns.

Marjorie appeared terrified. I think I was more indignant. 'What on earth do you want?' I shouted.

'We've come to search,' said one of the soldiers.

'Search? What for?' I asked.

'Guns,' he said. 'Ammunition.'

'Ammunition?' I repeated. 'What do you mean? We haven't got any ammunition.'

One of the soldiers stood over us, pointing his gun in our direction, while the other made a fairly thorough search of the bedroom and bathroom. I could sense that Marjorie was willing me not to react, and indeed her instincts were right because when I continued to protest, the gun was brought to within inches of my face.

The spectacle of two English ladies abroad suddenly confronted by soldiers with machine-guns may be amusing in theory, but in practice it was far from funny. Had we been caught up in a revolution? Is that why the street outside was lined with people? I hoped that no one was thinking of planting guns or ammunition on us. Who knows but we might have been required to sweep up the street after the crowds had gone? We need not have worried. Nothing was discovered, and that afternoon the President of Rumania and his entourage passed by our window so fast that, even had blinds not been drawn over the car windows, I doubt if any of the crowd could have spotted him. He was apparently on a State visit, and all buildings along the route had presumably also been visited by soldiers with machine-guns.

Eventful as our stay in the Philippines was turning out to be, nothing was as extraordinary as our firsthand experience of the work of the psychic surgeons – and of one in particular, Romy Bogorin.

As someone who had practised spiritual healing for many years, I was of course interested to learn as much as possible about the Filipino healers. Their reputation for supposedly miraculous cures had circulated around the world. There were several healers throughout the islands, the most famous being Tony Agpaoa. Friends of mine had gone to him to be healed and on one occasion I was part of a group of people who subscribed to send a young psychic to him who had a bad heart condition. I knew that a surprisingly large number of invalids, having given up hope of orthodox remedies, thought nothing of saving up and flying across the world to see him.

There were those however who claimed that Agpaoa and his followers were frauds and that they achieved some of their supposed results by sleight of hand; that they were conjurors rather than healers.

It had been arranged in advance for me to meet the brothers Romy and Joe Bogorin, and indeed our choice of hotel was dictated by the fact that the brothers had their surgery in the hotel. It had been agreed that I would take photographs of them at work and send a daily report, which I taped, back to London. Both Marjorie and I wanted also to consult them as patients. I had a minor problem with my chest and I was worried about the veins in one of my legs.

I thought it would be a good idea to see just how the Bogorins worked, so I went along as a patient without first contacting them. I went into their waiting room and was asked to complete a form about my medical condition and problems. Then I was asked to undress and go into the treatment room and lie on one of the couches. Marjorie was with me and was allowed to accompany me.

We entered the room and I lay on a couch as instructed. Marjorie sat on a chair at the side of the couch. The Bogorin brothers worked with two male assistants, and it was not unusual for them to be treating more than one patient simultaneously. On this occasion Romy, the elder brother, came in and introduced himself to me. He was a small man by British standards and wiry looking. He must, I thought, have been in his thirties. He was dressed in a short-sleeved white shirt and a pair of dark trousers.

He did not seem surprised that I had come for treatment as well as to investigate his activities, and he went to work immediately. He touched me with his hands, just as I had touched so many of my own patients over the years, and then he told me to turn over on my stomach. This rather surprised me because I had mentioned only my chest and my leg on the form, but he said that he felt that my neck was more important. I confess that I had had a slight problem with the back of my neck ever since the car accident in the West Indies many years before; on and off

99

I had had some treatment for it but I had come to live with it, so much so that I never thought to mention it on the form.

I do not know exactly what happened next. I felt dizzy, but not in any pain, and I vaguely remember seeing Romy Bogorin throw something bloody into a bowl. I distinctly remember Marjorie saying, 'Oh, my God!'

She later told me that Bogorin had opened the back of my neck and removed what looked like a blood clot. I asked her how he had done this, and she said that he had simply run his finger across the neck.

This may sound incredible, and the reader must believe it or not. All I will say is that Marjorie was a trained hospital matron who had been a theatre sister for many years, so her testimony cannot safely be disregarded.

After this amazing 'surgery', if that is what it was, I was given general healing over my whole body and then told to rest for three hours and to return for more general healing every day. The advice to rest was quite unnecessary because I could hardly have done otherwise; I was quite knocked out. And as for the neck, I felt a slight soreness for two days, after which I was very much better.

The next day it was Marjorie's turn for healing, and my opportunity to watch her being treated. I saw Romy put his hands up in prayer, say a few words in his own tongue presumably, and quickly touch her chest. To my astonishment – although I should perhaps have expected it after what Marjorie had told me – he appeared to open her chest and remove some tissue. I could not fathom how he had managed this.

When Marjorie next went for healing, Romy asked whether I, a healer myself, would like to open my friend's body. I was quite shaken. 'I couldn't possibly do that,' I said. 'We never do such things in England!' This sounds quite funny now but it serves to show what confusion I was in. I muttered something about it not being very hygienic.

He laughed and took hold of one of my fingers which he held in the air while he prayed. Then he placed my finger on Marjorie's body below her stomach.

I know that many readers will not believe me when I say that her body appeared to open at my touch. I admit that I was in a state of considerable shock. I heard Romy telling me, 'Pull it out, pull it out. Pull all that muck up,' and there was something peculiar in my hand. 'Throw it in the basin,' he instructed. Later Marjorie told me that she had felt something being pulled out, though just what it was – if not from her inside – I cannot possibly say. 'And now we'll close the body,' Romy said, placing my hands on the place where it had opened. Suddenly it was sealed again.

This experience was so extraordinary that had I not seen it with my own eyes, I would not have believed it. I am convinced that Romy Bogorin and others are genuine healers and not sleight-of-hand practitioners. I believe too that under his guidance I somehow performed the 'miracle' myself, though how I did it I just do not know, and I am sure that I could not do it alone to save my life.

There are those who will not believe me or who will say that I am deluding myself, but I can do no more than state what I believe to be the facts. There are other people – or perhaps the same ones – who do not believe, despite all the evidence, that I see and talk to spirit people. Many sensible people are only able to accept what they themselves experience.

Caution is always a good idea in these matters provided one keeps an open mind. It is very foolish however to close one's mind, particularly in the face of evidence, however bizarre. My own experience with a flying saucer is a case in point. Like most people, I have heard and read stories about unidentified flying objects for years, but until recently I had never seen one. As far as I was concerned, the evidence, although impressive, was inconclusive, but I did not

101

close my mind and say that because I had not seen such an object, it did not exist. On the contrary, I kept a truly open mind.

In August 1982 I was in Switzerland, the guest of Fred and Sylvia Pestalozzi who have a beautiful home on Lake Zurich. We were returning there after dinner at their daughter's house when something big and dark cast its shadow on the car. I was quite startled because of the suddenness but Fred, who was driving, said it was a large bird, probably an owl. I found this rather difficult to accept but reasoned that he lived in the district and must know that such birds existed.

Very shortly afterwards we arrived back and Fred put the car in the garage and shut the door. As we walked towards the house, an object appeared above us in the sky, about two hundred yards to our left, and disappeared before our eyes. All three of us saw it clearly. It was less a flying saucer than a flying cigar with a bright light at the front.

Just what it was I do not know, but that we saw it I am positive. It was undoubtedly a flying object of some kind, and it vanished instantly as if it had dematerialized. I shall sound even stranger to those who doubt me when I say that I have encountered other experiences of materialization and dematerialization, to which I shall refer later, and I realize that I may be challenging the reader's credulity in writing about healers who can open bodies with a finger, unidentified flying objects and materialization and dematerialization, one after the other. But I can only beg the reader to keep an open mind. It was not only I who saw the lighted cigar in the sky, and not only I who observed the Bogorins at work.

The psychic surgeons never use anaesthetics, but they seem never to cause pain despite the fact that they work in what by normal medical standards would be regarded as a very amateurish way. When I asked Romy Bogorin how he operated, he could only say that he and the other Filipino healers had trained very hard and that God worked through them. He could not explain his gift except to say that it had been passed down from his ancestors through many generations. In the village where he came from, there were no doctors, and in any case the people could not afford medical attention. There was always a healer, however, but he was regarded as no more remarkable than the local carpenter or housebuilder.

I speculated whether perhaps a very strange power emanated from the volcanic soil in the Philippine Islands. Curiously the possibility of this was suggested by a story I heard a few weeks later from a woman in Australia.

She told me that her jaw had been broken while she was having her wisdom teeth removed. Unfortunately the damage was thought to be very near the brain, so she said, and either she or her medical adviser was nervous about an operation, so she decided to wait to see if the jaw healed naturally. This must have been wishful thinking of a high order because she was in agony and could barely manage to eat anything but baby food. She was drinking a bottle of whisky a day, through a straw, to ease the pain.

She was told of a Filipino healer called Placido, and decided to visit him. She asked a friend to look after her daughter if she failed to return, saying that she did not intend to come back if they could not heal her in the Philippines.

On her first day in Manila she caught dysentery, and Placido said that he could not operate until she was cured of this complaint. He then took her and buried her in the volcanic sand, up to her neck, for twenty-four hours! The dysentery vanished and she felt amazingly fit, which surprised her enormously for she obviously did not know about the healing powers of volcanic sand which I believe are not unlike those of the Dead Sea for people with skin diseases.

103

The following day Placido was able to operate. This lady told me that he had placed a finger on her left cheek and she had felt a sort of click, and in his hand was a piece of bone. He had then performed similarly on the right cheek. 'Open your mouth,' he said, and nervously, because she had been unable to do so properly for months, she had tried to obey him. To her amazement, she had managed to open her mouth to its full extent, and the awful pain had gone. He told her that the relief would last for three years, after which time she should return for further healing. When I met her the three years were almost up and she was on her way back to see Placido. She had had no pain in the meantime.

This is only one of many such stories I have heard at first hand, but of course nothing was as convincing as the evidence of my own eyes. While we were in the hotel in Manila, a group of people – most of them in advanced stages of cancer – arrived from Britain. They had all been told that there was no hope for them, and they knew that they were grasping at straws. They looked like the walking dead. Two days later, after treatment from the Bogorins, they were all dancing in the ballroom. I cannot say whether their cure was permanent or temporary, but it was certainly as near miraculous as anything I have seen.

Perhaps the most amazing sight I have ever witnessed was an operation by Romy Bogorin, who appeared to remove a patient's eyes, lay them on the man's cheek, clean out the eye sockets with water and put the eyes back. I say 'appeared' to do so because I cannot explain it logically; commonsense tells us that one cannot remove the eyes from a human being as one can from a doll. And yet I do not think I imagined this; I am convinced I saw it.

It all happened so quickly that I could not tell how the feat had been performed, and I can well sympathize with any reader who thinks that I am gullible and easily deceived. People who know me well do not, I think, believe this of me, and I do not believe it of myself. I am sure I was watching a healer and not a magician. In any case Bogorin's record of successful cures could not possibly have been achieved by anyone but a genuine healer.

Fortunately Marjorie Horton was also present when this particular operation was carried out. She is a scientifically trained and sceptical person who, in her professional capacity, has witnessed hundreds of operations. She is a staunch witness to the facts I have reported. She believes that she saw what I believe that I saw.

# Chapter Eleven

My reception in Australia was no less enthusiastic than that in America. Americans are wonderfully warm people and generously hospitable. They *want* to like you. The Australians are no less warm and hospitable but they are perhaps less emotional. They are very down-to-earth, and in Australia you have to deliver the goods. Once you do so, however, there is no limit to their enthusiasm.

During ninety-four days of personal appearances at public meetings and on radio and television shows, I must have delivered the goods because I was rapturously received. Fortunately I am a down-to-earth person or the praise might have gone to my head. It is quite an experience – something I had not known before – to be given a standing ovation, and on more than one occasion. The first time in Melbourne I felt lifted out of myself, as light as air. Actors must know the feeling, but it took me by surprise. After all, I was only doing in Australia what I had been doing for years at home.

By the time I left Sydney for the last time on that visit, en route for New Zealand, I was exhausted but elated. My brother was called onto the stage and everybody sang 'Now is the hour for me to say goodbye'. It was a very emotional experience. Not as emotional however as our meeting in Brisbane over three months earlier.

When I got off the plane Fred was waiting for me with his wife and daughter. I had not of course seen him since I was a little girl, but I knew him immediately. He said he recognized me also, for I was very like my mother. Also waiting for me were several newspapermen and photographers, and almost before I could greet my brother we were whisked into the VIP lounge where I was interviewed for television. The story of the psychic from England who had discovered her long-lost brother in Australia was apparently very newsworthy. I could see that Fred was somewhat taken aback by what was happening. I warned the camera crews to take it easy in case he had another coronary!

Fred was absolutely delighted to have made contact again with a member of his old family after so many years, and his delight was shared by me and, I believe, by his wife and daughter. I stayed with them for a fortnight before embarking on the crowded programme that had been arranged for me. So much happened during the next few weeks that one event blurs in my mind with another, and the experiences that I vividly recall may not even be the most interesting. Don Davis, who was responsible for planning the tour, kept records of much that happened, and I have been able to refresh my memory by reference to him.

I think he was particularly impressed that I healed people by telephone or over the radio, and one particular story he recorded was that of a polio victim who had been in a wheelchair for seventeen years. This man had grown to accept his affliction but what he could not easily abide was the ceaseless and agonizing pain caused by the swelling of his knees. The pain never left him day or night. 'My knees are so swollen,' the man told Don, 'that my wife, when buying my clothes, has to slit my trousers from the bottom up to accommodate my knees, which are always four times their normal size.'

This man listened to me on the Mary Hardy Show, on which I was giving healing to telephone callers. Unfortunately he could not get through. Later in the day he saw me on television, on the Don Lane Show, on which I was giving clairvoyance. He suddenly became aware that the usual

107

pain in his knees was fading, and looking down he was amazed to see that his knees were both of normal size again.

Don Davis kept track of this man for nine months, and he records that during that time the pain never returned and that the swelling never reappeared.

This of course is an example of mass healing, or healing by remote control, because I had not been asked to heal this man – indeed I did not know of his existence – and I had not actually treated him or considered his problem. There was a similar case in Australia of a woman, unknown to me, whom I had apparently cured of hepatitis without knowing it. She followed me from Melbourne to Sydney to attest to this fact. Although this astonished her, it was well within my own experience. When I heal in public, at the end of a meeting I ask everyone to join hands. Somehow a tremendous energy and healing power are generated, and many times people have been healed instantaneously in such circumstances without my personally touching them.

Another similar example was the case of a Melbourne lady who wrote to me because, she said, she wanted to share with me her 'great personal miracle'. She had been to the dentist for a check-up before she had first seen me. Following a lengthy examination, she was told that she needed treatment, the nature of which the dentist noted on a card. He made an appointment for a later date and asked her to bring the card along with her.

She returned to his surgery on the appointed day, having in the meantime seen me on television and at a public meeting. In no way had she spoken or made contact with me except insofar as she was one of a very large audience at the Dallas Brook Hall. The dentist took her card and examined her mouth.

'What dentist have you been to since I gave you this card?' he asked.

'None,' she replied. 'Why do you ask?'

The dentist's reply staggered her. 'Everything on this card – and the work is extensive – is all done perfectly,' he said.

This lady put two and two together and decided that she had been cured by the mass healing at my meeting. I showed her letter to Don who asked me whether he might investigate further. I readily agreed, and he interviewed both the lady and the dentist, who was able to confirm the strange story – strange to some people, but not to me, because I have so much experience of this sort of thing.

I am occasionally affected more strongly than usual, and such an instance happened in Tasmania. My fame, such as it was, had been spread far and wide across the island by a certain reporter who had put me to the test as soon as I arrived in Hobart. He introduced me to his newspaper's photographer whose arm had been in a sling for months. He could hardly lift a book from the table without suffering pain. I was challenged to try my healing on him.

Now I cannot heal to order. I can only try, and what happens is beyond my control. As I have said so many times, God is the healer; I am only his channel. Through me, God has made the deaf hear, the dumb speak, the blind see and the crippled walk. But this does not mean that I am bound to succeed, and I did not like the idea of a challenge that might result in bad publicity if I failed. I agreed however to give healing to the photographer in the firm conviction that I would be able to help him.

Apparently the word had flashed around the newspaper offices because within minutes heads and faces appeared everywhere to watch the demonstration. This did not worry me because I am used to audiences. The reporter later wrote a full account of what happened. Apparently I took the photographer's hand in my left hand while I placed my right hand on his elbow. I then moved my hand up and down from the patient's shoulder to his wrist.

109

Then I bent his arm at the elbow and told him to pick up a chair.

He looked at me in astonishment as he tried to lift the chair, and in even greater astonishment as he achieved what he thought was an impossible feat. He lifted the chair higher and higher and said, 'My God, there is no pain. This is amazing.' The reporter then asked the man to lift a heavy table, which he managed to do with complete freedom and ease.

The report of this far from extraordinary incident may have had something to do with the fact that my next public meeting, in the Hobart University Theatre, attracted 1,500 people, of whom 500 had regrettably to be turned away. It has always been my habit to remain in the hall at the end of a meeting until the last of the audience has dispersed. At a healing meeting, there are usually some people in wheel-chairs, and this gives me an opportunity to talk to them.

It was in Hobart that I was much affected by meeting such a person. He had had a brain tumour removed and had been wheeled into the hall over uneven ground before the doors closed, causing him great pain. As Don Davis was ushering me through the empty aisles after the meeting, he saw the shadow of a wheelchair on the second landing. 'Oh, my Lord, Doris, I forgot,' he apologized. 'This man needs you desperately.'

I was very tired after three and a half hours on stage, but of course I went to the man. His wife had driven him many miles to see me, and his parents were also with them. He was partially paralysed and could not walk. Worse still, he could not speak. His wife said that he had not spoken for three years and so could not reply to me.

I placed my hands on his head, and prayed hard for the pain to be relieved. Don said later that my hands had trembled violently. I then put the forefinger of my right hand under his chin and lifted it up until I was looking into

110

his eyes. They were large and brown, and tears brimmed over his cheeks.

I looked straight at him and said, 'What are you going to say to me?' In retrospect this was a peculiar question to put to a man who could not speak, but I must have felt impelled to ask it.

I shall never forget the haunted look in his eyes as he opened his lips and somehow managed slowly to enunciate the words 'I – love – you.' The words were laboriously fashioned and uttered with meticulous precision.

'Oh, my God,' his wife said. 'He hasn't said that to *me* for seven years.' She was sobbing uncontrollably.

Whether the man's declaration was to me or his wife I could not be sure, but we both thought at the time that he was addressing me. So I asked him, 'And what are you going to say to your wife?'

He turned towards her and she embraced him. Then, in the same manner that he had spoken before, he said 'I love you too.'

For some reason this experience moved me more than most, and according to Don, who was present throughout, husband and wife, his mother and father, Don himself and I were all in tears.

Don travelled with me everywhere I went in Australia. Someone sent him a large box of grapefruit while we were in Toowoomba, and he said he would prepare and bring one into me in the morning before we went down to breakfast. I woke up at two o'clock in the morning with a strange feeling. I had left my handbag, which contained some jewellery, on a shelf by the television set, and something told me to move it. So strong was my presentiment that I got out of bed, fetched the bag and placed it between the two twin beds in my room. I went back to sleep.

In the morning, just as Don arrived with the grapefruit, two men in the corridor called out to him, 'Check all your belongings. We've been done. We've been robbed.' Sure enough all my luggage had been turned over in the middle of the night, but nothing was taken, presumably because there was nothing of value to take. The thief or thieves, who must have been prowling around my room while I was asleep, had missed the handbag and the jewellery either because it was in a dark place or because they did not want to come too near the bed.

I told Don that whoever had entered the rooms had a key, and that they would return. He laughed at me, but for two nights I pushed a table and chairs against the door before retiring for the night, which I put back in position in the morning before Don arrived with my grapefruit. On the third day Don told me that the thief had returned the night before and had been caught in the room next to mine by a farmer who was occupying the room with his wife. The arrested man was a boyfriend of one of the maids.

I have told this story because I thought it was about as near as I was likely to come to crime in Australia, but in fact I actually became involved in a murder case – in an indirect way, I hasten to add, on a later visit I made there. I was talking to a woman journalist when a lady appeared to me who gave her name and told me that she was the journalist's aunt. 'I lived in your country, not here,' she said, and told me that she had been murdered.

I asked the journalist if she had an aunt of that name. Not only was this so but the aunt had been killed six years before in England, near Bath, where she lived. The aunt then described to me what had happened. She had gone out shopping and, on return, had parked her car in the driveway of her house. There was a noise from the garage and she had gone to investigate. Two men were there who had hit her with an iron bar and some sort of axe, killing her. She said that she had lain there until her husband returned and found her.

The journalist was so impressed by what she regarded as this incredible description that she begged me to meet her mother, the dead woman's sister. I agreed to do so, and while I was talking to the mother, the dead woman appeared to me again and told me further details, including how distressed her husband had been when he found her dead body.

I forgot all about this, but one day when I was back home in London my husband telephoned to tell me that the Bath Murder Squad had been on to him. They had rung his office and said, 'Is your wife Doris Collins? We want to interview her.'

Preposterously, Philip replied, 'Good God, she's never murdered anybody!'

They reassured him. They only wanted to talk to me. The Australian journalist had apparently been in touch with the British police as a result of what I had told her, and they were following up their enquiries. Philip arranged for me to speak to a senior detective.

I asked him if he believed in clairvoyance. He said he had had no experience of it. He asked me whether I could again contact the murdered lady. 'I don't know that I can,' I replied. 'I can try, but it's not a case of just snapping my fingers and she'll come along.' Even while I was saying this, however, I began to hear her voice. 'She's here,' I said in triumph.

The detective asked me to obtain whatever information I could from her. She again explained how the murder had happened, and was able to give me descriptions of the house and the two men involved. 'Does this all make sense?' I asked.

His reply did not surprise me. 'If you'd have been at the scene of the crime,' he said, 'you couldn't have described it more accurately.'

He then asked me whether, if they arrested any suspects,

I would be prepared to identify them, by which he meant would I be able to say whether they fitted the descriptions given to me by the dead woman; I had not of course actually seen them.

I think I disappointed him when I said that that was not my function. It was one thing to pass on a message from the murdered woman; quite another to become her agent to track down her killers. That was a matter for her family perhaps and for the police. I could not be responsible for pursuing the criminals. Perhaps I felt not unlike a priest to whom a secret has been confided during confession.

The detective then asked whether I would talk to him again if there were any significant developments. I replied that I would wait until that time arrived and that then I would have to give the matter my consideration. It is my belief that we are all punished in one way or another for our bad behaviour, and I felt sure that the killers would be punished anyway, whether or not they were caught.

I never heard another word and did not have the curiosity to make further enquiries, but I assume that the murderers were not apprehended.

On another occasion, more recently, I found myself describing a murder. This was in the United States. I was appearing on a phone-in radio show in Boston, and a woman telephoned to ask what had happened to her son, who had disappeared two months before. All at once I received a very grim picture of a dead man lying in bushes near some water. He had been shot.

I was sure this was the woman's son, but how was I to tell her? I would never willingly forecast disaster but it is another matter to report something that has already occurred. I cannot remember my words, and no doubt they were as comforting as I could make them, but without saying more than was necessary, I told the woman that

114

her son was dead, hoping thereby to remove the uncertainty with which she had been living for the past few weeks.

I was lecturing at Boston University on the following Sunday when the woman approached me in person. She asked whether I could give her any further information. I told her what I had already seen, and then I had a picture of some men hitting the dead man over the head before pulling him out of his car and dragging him across the grass.

According to the woman, who was quoted in a local newspaper, I then told her that I could not go on thinking about her son's death. I had a very bad head. She also said that I became very nervous and that all I could say was 'God bless you, dear.'

My radio testimony caused a sensation locally, especially when a week later the dead man's body was discovered under a pile of leaves near a cranberry bog. He had been shot three times in the face. Once again, I do not know if the crime was ever solved, nor am I even curious. I only recall that the episode was very distressing to me – but my own distress was of course nothing to that of the family of the murdered man to whom I had, wittingly or otherwise, given news of the killing in public.

What am I supposed to do if somebody asks me point blank: Did my husband murder anybody? That astonishing question was actually put to me in New Zealand, where I went following my first visit to Australia. I took part on a Monday in a 'Talkback Show' on the radio, during which I dealt with telephone enquiries for over three hours. The response was exceptional, so much so that I was asked to return the following day. Apparently so many people tried to reach me on the second occasion that the Post Office appealed for restraint on the part of callers, who were jamming the exchange.

It was on this radio show that the extraordinary question

was posed. I did not of course know the caller or anything about her. I dealt with the question as I did with any other: I simply applied my mind to it and waited to see what came to me. In fact I received a very clear picture of a man, whom I described. The caller expressed astonishment, saying that I had given an accurate description of her husband, who had been convicted of a double murder and was serving a prison sentence. I interrupted her to say that he was innocent.

I cannot explain why I was so convinced of his innocence; it was just something I knew. And then I got somewhat carried away and, although I knew nothing of the circumstances, I started to say things about the murder which hit the headlines. I did not know what I was getting into; in cases like this, when I get going, something takes over and I either do not know what I am saying or do not care.

From newspaper reports I see that I told the caller that her husband had never been to the house of the murdered couple; that their bodies had been taken from the house on a truck or trailer; that there had been serious quarrels in their house the week before the killings; and that 'another woman' was involved in the murders. I also said that the convicted man was too simple-minded to have planned the murders and the removal of the bodies.

What attracted most attention however was my claim that a cartridge case had been planted outside the house of the murdered couple. It was this cartridge case that had been used by the Prosecution with such effect to convict my caller's husband, but if he were not responsible for it being there, if indeed it had been planted, this – together with other matters – might put a different complexion on the issue of his guilt or innocence.

For once I do know the end of the story, though not the details. The local police chief was among the listeners to the programme, and either because of what I had said – and of

116

course I knew nothing about the circumstances at the time – or for other reasons also, he caused further enquiries to be made, as a result of which there was a retrial and my caller's husband was finally acquitted.

# Chapter Twelve

Gordon Dryden was the host on the New Zealand Talkback Show that brought me a measure of fame in Auckland. Towards the end of my second appearance on his programme, a young man came in and sat down. When we went off the air, Gordon introduced me to him. 'This is Johnny Walker,' he said.

The only Johnny Walker I knew was the colourful gentleman on the whisky bottle, from which my readers will realize that I am no sportswoman or follower of sport. The last thing I am likely to do is to turn on the television on Saturday afternoon to watch football.

'Oh, yes,' I said. 'How very nice to meet you.'

'He's our hope for the Olympics,' Gordon went on. 'He's our champion mile record breaker.'

I looked at the great athlete, of whom I am ashamed to say I had never heard, and said: 'You're going to have rather a problem, aren't you?'

'What do you mean?' he asked.

'You've got a very painful knee,' I answered. 'It's causing you a lot of problems with your running.'

'How do you know?' he said, for it was not public knowledge.

'I've been on this programme now for two or three hours as a psychic,' I replied. 'That's how I know.'

The young man then told me that he had been unable to train as he wished for many weeks. He had been everywhere to obtain help, but the medical advice he had received had not effected a cure, and he was worried.

118

It was then that Gordon challenged me to see what I could do. 'You're a healer, Doris,' he said. 'Heal him.'

I agreed to try if the athlete himself wanted me to. He looked cautious. 'What are you going to do?' he asked.

'I don't know,' I said, 'until I start.'

He obviously thought there was nothing to lose, and Gordon conducted us to a little room upstairs. I put my hand on the young man's knee and he shook all over, as if with fear – although I am sure that was not the reason. After some minutes he told me that the pain had gone, and he jumped up and did some exercises. 'I haven't been able to do these for weeks,' he said.

Shortly afterwards, emitting a triumphant yell, he bounded down the stairs into the broadcasting studio, and called out: 'Gordon, she's for bloody real!'

I knew this was a compliment indeed. He then did more exercises and asked me whether the cure would last. I was certain it would and told him so.

Back in England three months later, I turned on the television on Saturday afternoon to look at an old film. The set was tuned to a channel that was featuring sport, and I saw a runner in a black vest streak across the screen. 'I know that boy,' I called out to Philip. My husband looked up. 'That's John Walker,' he said, 'the New Zealand champion. He's just broken the world record for the mile.'

John Walker later told the story from his point of view to an American reporter. He admitted that for two years before he met me, he had had chronic pain in his knee after hard training; the knee would swell and he would have difficulty in straightening his leg. It did not bother him during races, but it was bad in the morning when he got up, during training and after races.

'Mrs Collins put her hands on my spine and on my knees,' he said. 'I felt vibrations coming through her fingertips. It was uncanny, incredible. Then after about five

119

minutes, she asked me to stand up and there was no more pain.

'The next Saturday I ran 400 metres fifteen times. If my knee was going to hurt, it would have hurt then. The next day I ran a seventeen-miler. No trouble!'

He thought I was 'astounding'. 'She certainly did me a lot of good,' he said, 'even though I don't really know what she did. No other kind of treatment worked for me.'

Philip told me the following year that Johnny Walker had won a gold medal at the Olympic Games in Montreal.

He was not the only athlete I encountered in New Zealand. In fact I met more sportsmen there than I had come across anywhere else. Another was Dick Quax. He had been one of New Zealand's greatest runners for a number of years, having won a silver medal in the 1,500 metres event at the Edinburgh Commonwealth Games five years earlier. At the time of my visit, although he had just recently won the New Zealand 5,000 metres title, the press and public were beginning to write him off as a world-class athlete. What they may not have known is that he had become beset by injuries that later necessitated operations on both legs.

He heard me on the car radio and came storming into the studio, expressing his determination, I was told, to 'get some of this', by which I suppose he meant some healing. Unfortunately healing does not come in bottles. I did not in fact see him; I was unaware who he was or even that he wanted to see me.

If I believed in coincidence – which I do not, for there are no coincidences – I would now say that by coincidence, as I was being driven to Auckland airport, we stopped at traffic lights. As we did so, a car drew up in the next lane and stopped a few yards ahead of us. The driver of the car said, 'That's Dick Quax, one of our top athletes.'

For some reason I said, 'He's going to be very good. In

**My Father**
Cooper by name and
master cooper by trade

**My Mother**
She was forty-eight when
I was born

**My Sister Emmie**
Her appearance from the
spirit world changed my
whole life

**Little Doris**

**Aged Twenty**
Just before my first
marriage

**Family Portrait** *back row (l. to r.)* My daughter-in-law Irene and my son Brian; myself and Philip; son Brian's elder daughter Susan; Margaret's husband Jim *front row* Mr and Mrs Perry (our friends); my daughter Margaret; my stepson Brian's wife Valerie and my stepson

**My Brother Fred in Brisbane** I had not seen him since I was a little girl

**Clint Walker in California**
"Cheyenne" cleared the stage for me

**Frankie Howerd Smiles** I am happy that I also know his more serious side

**Greeting Michael Bentine** Who could ask for a better friend?

**Peter Sellers Pays
Tribute**
He was guest of
honour at our dinner-
dance

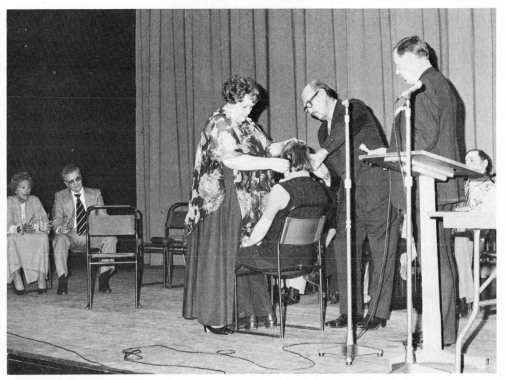

**Healing in London** Fanny Cradock and Michael Bentine look on while Johnny
Cradock and my husband Philip assist me

**Demonstrating in America** *above* Clairvoyance in a Los Angeles church
*below* Healing in California, assisted by a well-known local healer

**Communicating with Karl May** The sitting at which the German writer told me
about himself for the film that was being made of his life. On the right is the actress-
photographer who took the picture of me working

**At the Royal Albert Hall**
Two studies of me at work

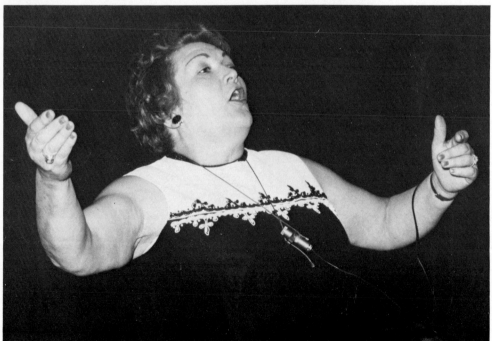

fact next year he will be world class.' This was the opposite of what most people thought; popular opinion was that he had been world class but was on the decline. Next year was the year of the Olympic Games, and I seemed to be forecasting success for him at the top level at the time of the Games.

My friend, who was driving the car, followed athletics and he also believed in me. He therefore watched Dick Quax's career with special interest. A top professional coach told him that Quax's training was going very well and that he was 'real medal material'. Quax actually ran within a tenth of a second of the world record for 5,000 metres. When he failed to qualify however in the 10,000 metres event at the Olympic Games, my friend thought that I had been exaggerating.

He reported however that as Dick Quax crossed the line to gain the silver medal in the 5,000 metres race at the Games, I was the first person he, my friend, thought of. He made the amusing remark that my clairvoyance was just as good at a busy intersection as at the radio studio!

I helped yet another athlete in New Zealand. A man wrote to say that he had seen me healing on a public platform, and could I help him? He was a former professional golfer who had had to give up the game. Would I heal him if he came to my next meeting?

This request put me in a difficulty. It is one thing to give healing privately, and quite another to do so in public. What I mean by this is not that the technique is different but that I cannot give priority to an individual in a public place. It is not like booking a seat at the theatre. The way I work is to select people, usually from those who come forward at a meeting, whom I feel impressed to heal. Sometimes I will be moved to go to someone in the audience who has not come forward, someone in a wheelchair for example.

121

There is always a time at a healing meeting when I invite people who require healing to come to the platform if they are willing and able. Usually there is such a rush that I have to employ stewards to keep control. I normally select fourteen or fifteen members of the audience, with whom I deal in turn.

I had replied regretfully to the golfer that I could not treat him differently from any other member of my audience, and I did not know whether he would be there at my next meeting. Again, by one of those coincidences in which I do not believe, he was one of a dozen or so people among literally hundreds who approached the stage whom I selected for treatment.

When his turn came, he introduced himself as the golfer who had written to me. His name was Ross Newdick. 'You refused to see me,' he said.

There were around 3,000 people in the hall. 'It's strange that I should have picked you out,' I replied. He said that he had a serious problem with his back and one of his legs. He could no longer drive a club, so had given up golf and had opened a liquor store. I gave him healing and then said, 'Imagine you've got a golf club in your hands. Now, drive!'

He went through the motion, cautiously at first and then apparently effortlessly. In great excitement, he jumped up, kissed me, told me he felt no pain and that he was better. I believe that he later returned to his career as a golfer.

To me, as I have said, all patients come alike and it does not matter if they are famous or unknown. During my work as a clairvoyant I have been consulted by very many well-known people, and I will have a word or two to say about some of these later in the belief perhaps that the reader would rather hear about Peter Sellers than about Mr Jones next door, although the experiences of Mr Jones are probably equally interesting and equally valid. Another reason to write about the famous is that people take notice of them. If Mrs Smith says something about me, no one beyond her own circle is likely to know; but if someone like Douglas Bader has something to say, it will probably find its way into the columns of the *Daily Telegraph*.

What I cannot, and will never, do is to reveal confidences, and I can only write about people who have themselves publicized my work or who have authorized me to refer to them. The stories of the three athletes in New Zealand have been widely reported. There are one or two other healing stories concerning well-known people that I feel able to write about.

One concerns the actress, Anna Polke. In her case cancer of the breast had been diagnosed when she consulted me. She did not want orthodox medical therapy, and although I told her not to ignore medical advice, I agreed to help her insofar as I could. To my delight – and more of course to hers – after several sessions the lumps on her breast disappeared. A year later a lump appeared on the other breast which, after healing, disappeared also. But she was naturally worried about the possibility of the problem spreading, and she was being urged by her specialist to go into hospital for exploratory surgery. She asked my advice, and I told her that only she could make the decision. She decided to take the medical advice and underwent the surgery. Nothing was found.

I draw no particular conclusion from this, and do no more than report the facts. Spiritual healing is now becoming more widely acceptable to the medical profession itself, and is a matter of study among scientists and religious thinkers. Recently I was one of twenty healers who devoted a weekend to discussing the subject with the monks of Worth Abbey in Sussex.

It was a most interesting occasion. The Benedictine Abbot of the monastery was a charming and intelligent man who related the story of how he had been asked to heal a

123

woman who sought his help during a visit to Lourdes. In such circumstances, it was his practice to pray, but on this occasion he instinctively laid his hands on the woman's head as he prayed. He was astonished at the relief in her condition. 'Something happened then,' he admitted, 'which I did not understand. I have tried to dismiss the incident, but I know it is my duty to come to terms with this knowledge.'

He expressed the view that in a community of men who had chosen a life-style of compassion, love and faith, there must be the possibility that within the community certain of the monks have a healing gift.

One of the younger monks pointed out that a carpenter named Jesus had laid his hands on people and healed them. 'His instruction,' he said, 'was not only to go out and preach but also to heal.'

It was then that I was invited to demonstrate my healing, and I began with the Abbot himself. I diagnosed an arthritic condition in his right knee, and he admitted that he did not have full mobility in the knee. After healing, he said that he had felt energy enter his leg, which within minutes seemed more mobile.

I realized that he himself was a healer, and told him so. I think he was more surprised however when I passed on to him a message from his mother, who appeared to me as I was healing him and who talked to me about her son. He told me that what I had related was completely accurate.

I next treated a retired army officer with an arthritic left hip that caused one of his legs to be shorter than the other. Following my healing, the legs became equal in length. I believe that the monks were impressed, and they asked me questions about technique. I told them that healing had to be simple. 'You must not get bogged down with detail,' I said and, referring to the celebrated healer Harry Edwards, I pointed out that he just rolled up his sleeves and got on with it. 'That's what you must do,' I added.

There was an amusing ending to my visit to Worth Abbey. One of the monks came up to me and asked whether I could spare him ten minutes or so. 'What for?' I asked. His reply made me laugh. 'The Abbot,' he told me, 'said the healing was wonderful but the fortune-telling was fantastic. I want some of what you gave him!' Fortune-telling it was not; but I knew what he meant.

Another well-known person who described healing as wonderful was the mime artist, Adam Darius. He sent the young dancer Kazimir Kolesnik to me for treatment on an injured foot. The young man had been told that the injury would take six months to heal but he was able to dance properly again after only nine weeks. He believed that I was responsible for his startling improvement.

Shortly afterwards Adam himself came to me. During the fitting of a contact lens, the cornea of his right eye had become badly scratched. He was in great pain when he was taken to hospital, where the swollen eye was bandaged. He had to keep both eyes shut because when he opened his good eye, he could not help opening the bad one too. He was therefore virtually sightless and could not go out without assistance.

He was very depressed, not knowing whether he would be able to fulfil his international engagements. He was led into my house for healing. He left under his own steam. His eye was still bloodshot and felt as though it were full of sand, but at least it was open. Within four days the scratch had completely gone, to the surprise of the doctors.

I received letters from both Kazimir and Adam, thanking me for what I had done for them. 'I have in my repertoire,' Adam Darius wrote, 'an item entitled "The Cripple and the Madonna", based on a tale of miraculous healing. When you opened my eyes, your face was indeed that of the Madonna.'

Doris Collins the Madonna! What a charming, if undeserved, compliment – but I must not allow that sort of thing to go to my head. I am a little embarrassed even to report some of the compliments that have been paid to me, but perhaps I may be allowed the indulgence of quoting just one more – not this time from a famous personality but from a Swiss gentleman, Willy Roosli, now my good friend. He is not English but I have not altered his language, because I think it is so delightful. I wish I could speak his language as well as he speaks mine. This is what he wrote:

'In January 1981, Mr Roosli felt a strong pain in his knee.

'The pain was so strong that he felt the knee would split.

'He went to a doctor. He told Mr Roosli there would be no chance of getting better.

'About twelve electro-shock therapies followed. After that, the pressure on the side was still there – and very painful. So the doctor told him to deal with it for the rest of his life.

'Mr Roosli heard about Doris Collins.

'In June 1981, Mr Roosli had a healing.

'The day after the healing he was able to play football and has continued to take part in all sports with no more pain ever since.'

Could one ask for a better testimony?

# Chapter Thirteen

οϵοοϵοοϵο

Although I have always been interested to learn as much as possible about my psychic gifts, I have accepted them as a matter of fact, just as I have accepted that I am large rather than small. I have not gone out of my way to enquire into the mysteries of the universe, and if I have more than average knowledge of some of the stranger aspects of existence, this is because they have been revealed to me.

Most of us believe that there are good and bad forces in the world, and it is far better if possible to concentrate on all that is good in life. I had never myself wanted to investigate the phenomenon of evil, and I am not sure that I would have accepted a particular invitation I received in 1947 had I known what it involved.

I was asked to examine a black box and, through clairvoyance, to give whatever information I could about it. I knew nothing about it, who owned it or what it contained, but I got a strong picture of an evil man who had died. I felt that he had been strongly influenced by sex, sometimes of an abnormal nature. He had had piercing, hypnotic eyes which gave him unusual power over people. Not only could he affect their health, but he had destroyed some of those who had opposed him.

This man had been connected with some sort of religious order – I saw the ritual garments – and indeed some of his followers had regarded him as a holy man. Unknown to his wife, he had practised 'black magic' rituals, locking himself up in a private room for the purpose.

The contents of the box included his writings on black magic and other subjects; I saw that quite clearly. There was also a beautifully coloured object that I could not identify.

I began then to get some very disturbing messages. The dead man, who told me he had died a recluse, insisted that he did not want the box opened. He wanted the contents destroyed. Several times he said that the box should remain closed. He went on to say that people had opened it against his wishes and that they had become ill or had been involved in accidents. He then threatened that he would strike down anybody who tried to open the box. He kept telling me that he had sold his soul to the Devil.

What I said was recorded at the time by Tom Johanson, who was one of the people present on this occasion. Apparently the box – more like a small trunk – had come into the possession of publisher Colin Smythe. It had once belonged to a man whom the *Sunday Mirror* called 'the evil archbishop' and I have subsequently seen photographs of him in archbishop's regalia – although he was no more an archbishop, at least not of any recognized church, than I am. Two men who had opened the box had met with serious mishaps in unusual circumstances; and two hard-bitten journalists had become violently sick while inspecting the box. It had been rumoured that the mere presence of the box in a room produced headaches, dizziness and depression.

Despite the warnings I had passed on from the dead man – and of course I knew nothing at the time about him or about the circumstances concerning the box – it was decided to open it. It was placed in the middle of the room in Colin Smythe's office, and the task of opening it was given to Tom Johanson, who wore rubber gloves for the purpose. He insisted too that I wore rubber gloves when it came to examining the contents.

As the lid was raised, I was conscious of a swirling sensation. Others present reported a feeling of giddiness,

128

and one observer felt a sharp pain at the back of the head. I swear that on two occasions the box moved away from me.

When I looked inside, I saw masses of books, notebooks, documents, charts and photographs. I was not interested in inspecting them too closely. At the very bottom was an envelope. It contained a brightly coloured sash.

Fortunately nobody experienced anything worse than a slight sickness or headache from opening this 'box of evil', but that it was surrounded by – indeed permeated with – something bad and unhealthy I was quite certain.

I was to come into contact with evil in a much more positive way when I visited South Africa four years later, but I did not seek it out. I do not believe in associating deliberately with evil people if I can help it, but evil is unfortunately a fact of life – sometimes I think it is good gone astray – and it is perhaps not very surprising that so many books are written and published nowadays about omens, possession and the like. They may be amusing to read about, but not to encounter.

I worked in Johannesburg, Pretoria, Port Elizabeth and Cape Town, usually giving joint demonstrations in public of clairvoyance and healing. It was for me a very interesting experience. I stayed at first with an English lady in Johannesburg. She had a maid, aged about forty, who was especially helpful to me. On my third day, the maid brought in my morning tea as usual and said to me: 'You're a witchdoctor.'

I was not sure whether this was meant as a compliment or a reproach, and I said, 'What makes you think that?'

'I feel it,' she replied.

'I don't deal with witchcraft,' I said.

'No, you're a good witchdoctor,' was her comment. 'I feel you do good things.' I was soon to learn that many South African black people have a highly developed natural psychic sense.

129

The maid confided to me that she had children whom she had left in the charge of her mother in her native village. I used to watch her every morning carrying a pail of water from the house to a hut in the garden. I mentioned this to my hostess, who told me that the hut was where the maid lived; in accordance with the local custom, she did not sleep in the house. I was somewhat curious.

'What is the hut like?' I asked.

'You won't be allowed to go in,' I was told. 'They don't like it.'

The following Sunday I met a black woman, beautifully if rather colourfully dressed in all her finery, and wearing dark glasses. I did not at first recognize the maid. I asked my hostess if the woman's eyes were bad. 'No,' she said, 'that's the fashion. She's got up for Sunday church.'

The next morning I told the maid how nice she had looked and how pretty her clothes were. This seemed to please her, for she said: 'When Madam's out, would you like to see my clothes?'

I thought she would bring them to me, but no – she meant me to visit her in her quarters. In view of what I had been told, I felt very privileged.

The hut was little more than an outhouse in the garden, serving as a sort of bedsitting room. There was no running water that I could see; hence the morning pail. The furniture was comfortable and practical rather than elegant, but there was a good quality bed. What puzzled me was that it had been raised on bricks instead of standing in its natural place on the floor. I asked the reason but the maid made no reply. Something told me that the subject must be taboo, so I let the matter drop.

During my stay in Johannesburg I was allowed four days' holiday which I spent largely in Kruger National Park, with a marvellous Scotsman called Crow as my guide and driver of the Jeep. It was extremely hot and we used to get up very early, as soon as day broke, to watch the animals feeding. It had been a lush season, which meant that the animals did not need to come out very much, so from the point of view of animal-watching it was not one of the most successful experiences. As if to make up for this, Mr Crow talked – and how he talked! He had lived in the country for many years and was a mine of information and full of stories. At one point he told me that he had one or two friends who were witchdoctors, and this of course put me in mind of the bed on bricks. I asked him about it.

'Oh, that's easy to explain,' he said. 'That's because of the *tokoloshe*.' He described the *tokoloshe* (sometimes spelt differently) as a sort of bogeyman whom many Africans believed was sent by a bad witchdoctor to grab them by the throat in the middle of the night. If they raised their beds off the ground, the creature could not get at them.

Investigations that I subsequently made indicate that the *tokoloshe* is usually a serpent-like creature, variously described as dwarf-like, half man and half subterranean. The important thing about him is that he is supposed to be the servant or agent of a person who casts evil spells. There are actually people who, for a fee, will cast such spells.

If someone seeks revenge, for example, he can go to a spell-casting witchdoctor – sometimes called the *umthakathi* – who may perhaps give him something to plant in or near the house of his enemy. This object, supposed to carry the power of the spell, is called *muthi* or *muti*, probably from the Zulu word *umuthi*, meaning medicine. There is good and bad *muthi*.

Some of this knowledge came in useful when I encountered the Crab Lady. I hope she will not mind the name I gave her but comparison with a crab was irresistible when I first saw her. This was at a public meeting in Johannesburg where she was being led down the aisle between the seats towards the platform. She came as near to walking sideways

131

as was possible, and the stewards did not have an easy task in helping her forward.

They eventually placed her in the front row of the audience, and as I made contact in thought, I picked up some very strange feelings. There was something very evil about the woman.

I was asked to heal her but I was so worried by her aura that I did something I had never done before. I refused to allow her on the platform.

'But she's come for healing,' the chairman of the meeting protested.

'I'm sorry,' I insisted. 'I will heal her if I can, but not in public. I'll see her after the meeting has finished.'

The meeting proceeded satisfactorily although I could not entirely dismiss the Crab Lady from my mind. She was there in the front row, slightly to my right, and staring me in the face every time I cast a glance in her direction.

In due course, as people started to leave the hall, I went down to her. I do not always want to know what is wrong with people who come to me for healing; I prefer to work as I feel impressed to do, and sometimes knowledge of what is apparently wrong can inhibit my dealing with what is actually wrong. I have discovered that many people who think they have one sort of problem in fact have another, and even the best medical diagnosis will not necessarily reveal the cause of the trouble. People will usually tell me what is wrong, or supposed to be wrong, with them; but I very rarely ask. In the case of the Crab Lady however, I felt it necessary to know something about her condition; I sensed perhaps that it was beyond my previous experience.

A number of things were told me but somehow I did not accept them as being accurate. So I started to give the woman healing in the usual way. She was middle-aged and white, and she stood up as I placed my hands in hers. Immediately I had a feeling in my bones that there was evil present, confirming even more powerfully what I had thought on first seeing her.

I may have sensed evil before but I had never touched it. One of the interesting facts that Mr Crow had told me was that, according to a witchdoctor of his acquaintance, if one feels oneself to be touching evil, putting alcohol on one's hands will act as a protective barrier. Little had I thought that this strange advice would come in useful so quickly. It is a measure of the strong impression of evil that emanated from the Crab Lady that I actually called out to Mr Crow, who had been in the audience, to get me some alcohol.

No one turned a hair. Perhaps the few people remaining in the hall thought I was an alcoholic, but I could not have cared less. A lady, who was standing nearby, may have known what I had in mind, for she handed me a small bottle from her handbag. 'Here is some perfume,' she said.

'That's alcohol, isn't it?' I said, sprinkling some of the liquid on the palms of my hands, before again taking the Crab Lady's hands in mine.

Immediately she became wildly violent and started to kick me. A torrent of words issued forth from her mouth. Although I did not understand them – she was, I later learnt, shouting and screaming in pure Zulu, a language that she did not normally speak or understand! – it was clear from her manner of utterance that she was swearing and cursing me.

Her outburst was so extraordinary that everybody still in the hall turned round. I knew there was an evil spirit in this woman. It was no figment of the imagination.

'I demand you leave this woman,' I said, addressing the spirit.

The woman continued to struggle to free herself from my grip; but I would not let go of her hands. To my horror she dropped flat on the floor. I thought for a terrible moment that she was dead, that I had killed her. I had never

133

experienced anything like this and I was inwardly terrified, although I tried not to show it.

I watched her closely. There was no movement. And then suddenly I saw that she was breathing and I thanked God. She opened her eyes and actually smiled at me! Then she got to her feet as though nothing had happened and said, quite simply, 'Thank you.' I could hardly believe the evidence of my eyes. A few minutes before she had been possessed; now she seemed quite normal. Gaining courage, I asked her to walk. She did so, as straight as could be; no longer did she move sideways like a crab.

I took her aside and spoke to her privately. She knew about her possession by an evil spirit and told me a story which at the time astonished me but which I have come to realize may not be as uncommon as at one time I thought.

The Crab Lady had gone to keep house for a farmer, a widower with two children. After a time, he married her, and the marriage was reasonably happy until the man died suddenly, whereupon the sons accused her of poisoning their father.

They did everything they could to make her life imposs-ible. Convinced that she had killed their father, they went to the authorities and the body was exhumed, but it was established beyond doubt that the man had died of natural causes. She heard from a friend that they had also been to a local witchdoctor.

She began to feel very ill and could not cope with the farm, so left and took a job as a caretaker. Unfortunately she kept falling asleep and started to speak in a language that her friends did not understand, and then began to walk in the crab-like fashion I had observed. Her doctor could neither diagnose her trouble nor help her. She had a strong feeling that she had been cursed by her stepsons and, having heard of my work, came to me in the full belief that I alone could cure her. Two years later I received a letter in which she told me that she was now healthy and able to continue with her work. There had been no recurrence of her distressing symptoms.

I was very interested in the Crab Lady's extraordinary story, and I discussed it with a number of experts in South Africa. I was told other stories about manic hysteria possessing women, notably girls who had turned down a man's proposal of marriage and who had become victims of an evil spell purchased by the malicious or jealous rejected suitor.

It became quite obvious to me that I had removed some sort of curse from the victim of an evil witchdoctor. I am aware that there is evil in the world and that there are evil people. It is known that I believe in reincarnation and I have often been asked what I think happens to such people after death. My instinct tells me that they must be surrounded by great darkness. If they never had an understanding of good in this life, they do not suddenly become angels when they pass over. I believe that we pass into the state of existence of which we have an understanding. We have to earn our places in the higher states, and death will not automatically put us there. However dark our situation, we can get into the light if we wish, because eternal progression is open to every soul. No man is left without a helping hand as long as he reaches out to the great source of all life.

In the meantime we have to struggle against evil, and I was highly gratified that I had been able to release this lady, especially since she was in no way responsible for the distressing condition.

I was learning more and more about the strange powers of the witchdoctors in South Africa. Some certainly worked for evil, but there were many more who worked for good. I asked if I might meet a benevolent one.

Through several enquiries I was taken to the house of a white nurse who had contact with such a person. She had

135

asked him if he would see me and he agreed; in fact he was waiting for me at the house when I arrived. He was a short, stocky man who spoke broken English, and I spent nearly two hours with him. He had a little black bag, containing his *dolos*. These were the symbols by which he read the future. They consisted mostly of animal bones and stones. He asked me first to touch them through the bag and then to hold them in my hands. Then he threw the bones on the floor, as one might throw dice, picking them up and throwing them again and again. Each time he studied the patterns they made on the floor. He started to tell me interesting things about myself, all of which were basically true. This, I am sure, was his way of receiving clairvoyance. Indeed he told me we had the same gift. The nurse assured me that she had told him nothing about me. He went on to say it was my destiny, not my choice, to work for people, and that this had been decided before I returned to earth this time. 'You have very heavy blood,' he said, and explained that this meant healing power. He forecast that I would continue to travel widely, but my life would never be really easy because the pathway of service is a lonely one, and I had decided to work largely alone, rather than in groups, because that way I achieved the best results.

He then went into the garden to get something for my protection, and coming back with a piece of bark from a tree, he told me to put it in distilled water and to drink a little each day. 'It will give you great strength,' he said. The nurse looked astonished. 'You're so lucky,' she told me. 'They never give their secrets away.'

I have still got the bark, but I confess that I have never had the courage to use it. My visit to the witchdoctor however had another practical outcome. For years I have been aware of many helpers from the spirit world. One of these is a Zulu, who has assisted me enormously with my healing work. A helper or guide is no more than an

136

assistant. Just as a business executive will employ a secretary, a telephonist and a receptionist to help him, so I have people who help me in different capacities, as I shall explain further in the next chapter. My Zulu guide, a big man who always gave me tremendous strength, first came to me in my early days as a medium, when I worked a great deal in trance. He used to greet me with the words '*Vula*' or '*Vula Momba*'. Neither I nor my students knew what this meant; we had always assumed that he was either saying hello or giving his name.

Now, when the witchdoctor went into the garden to fetch the bark, he closed the French windows behind him; and when he returned a few minutes later, finding them shut, he called out to my hostess, the nurse, '*Vula, vula!*' I was quite startled to hear the word again. When the nurse had let him in, I asked the witchdoctor: 'What did you say?'

'*Vula*,' he replied. 'It means to open.'

I told him about my guide, and he explained that Momba was probably his name – there is a River Momba in Tanzania – and that what he had been saying to me was probably, 'Open yourself to Momba to work with you.'

It had taken me all these years and a visit to Africa to have this revealed to me!

# Chapter Fourteen

❍◯∞◯∞◯∞◯❍

It was in 1979, not long after returning from South Africa, that Doris Stokes and I were honoured by being named Spiritualist of the Year by *Psychic News*. I was given a silver goblet, suitably inscribed, and a signed testimony in recognition of my work as a psychic over forty years. It was highly unusual – perhaps unique – for two people to receive the citation in one year, and I remember thinking that if I deserved it at all, it was as much for my healing work as for anything else.

The truth is, I suppose, that I cannot put clairvoyance and healing in completely separate compartments. I am probably using my clairvoyant powers automatically while I am giving healing. Indeed, in my early days, I used to heal in trance. I find now that my healing is just as effective without the need to let someone take over my personality, which is what happens in trance. Years ago people were more impressed by trance healing, but I now prefer to retain my personality and I very rarely need to go into trance to achieve results.

I have already spoken about my Zulu guide. I also have a medical guide, who used often to be there in spirit to help me when I was healing – and I did not have to trance for him to appear. I was first given him by George Daisley, a psychic who now lives in California, at a public meeting in Ilford. I must have been in my middle twenties at the time and I was in the audience when George, who used to write backwards so that what he wrote had to be held up to a mirror, said he had a message for me. We had not met before and were unknown to each other. 'I've got to go to

138

this lady,' he announced, pointing at me. 'I've a message for her from a doctor who works with her.'

George said that the sender was using his, George's, hand to dictate to him, and when the message was recorded he held it up to the large mirror, which was always one of his 'props', and I read it. It was signed Dr Carl Klein, who told me that he would continue to work with me and that I would go all over the world to do God's work.

I do not think I had been aware of Dr Klein before that time, but since he spoke of continuing to help me, I was obviously no stranger to him. Later I was told that while I was in trance, he sometimes spoke through me. He told my students that he was a German Jew who had been tortured by the Nazis because he refused to work for them. I was so interested in this that I made enquiries in Germany and learnt that there was such a doctor of that name from Berlin who had been in a concentration camp.

I have seen him often since – a slight man in his late fifties, usually wearing a pince-nez or sometimes gold-rimmed glasses, and occasionally (but not always) sporting a moustache. He appears to me much less frequently nowadays, but I very often *feel* his presence while I am healing. He is my greatest helper and guide.

People often ask me how I go into trance and what then happens. As to how, it is a knack that I either acquired or with which I was graced. I can sometimes do it very quickly, almost like pressing a switch. I concentrate, trying to go into oblivion. I try to think of nothing, or else of pleasant things such as walking on a beach and hearing the sea, until I feel detached from the world.

I believe that there are several degrees of trance – probably five. The first is an awareness of another personality, and at that stage I can still hear myself speak, although words are put into my mouth. Gradually I lose more and more of myself until I am completely taken over.

139

Beyond that I cannot remember a thing, and I have to rely on observers to tell me what I said or did.

Under controlled conditions, my students have stuck pins in me while I have been in trance, and I have felt nothing. In such a state I become the other personality as near as possible, and sometimes take on his or her voice. Occasionally my face – and even my body – changes. I know this from a whole mass of evidence but perhaps one of the most interesting examples is the following, attested by my husband Philip. Soon after our marriage we were in our flat near the seafront in Worthing. Although Philip had been my student, we did not deal with psychic matters during our spare time. He was reading one sunny Sunday afternoon while I was sewing. I began to feel very drowsy, and shut my eyes. Philip tells me that I said to him, 'I feel very strange. When I come round give me a glass of water. I don't want you to shake me.' The implication is that I knew I was going into a trance without intending to.

Philip, who was of course aware of my psychic powers, was quite amazed when suddenly my features changed completely and there in my place was his mother! My features had been transfigured and my personality overshadowed by a woman of utterly different appearance. More amazingly, I appeared to be dressed in the style that his mother had affected. I then spoke to him in his mother's voice – or, more accurately perhaps, she spoke to him through me, reminding him of the time when they had lived over his father's shop in Cheshire and of the happy days they and Philip's two sisters had spent at the seaside. She sent her love to the girls.

I had never discussed his childhood with Philip. The message had some significance for him because the family had owned a chalet on the beach in the Wirral Peninsula, and their Sunday beach lunches were a highlight of the children's lives. When I came round, Philip fetched the glass of water that I had requested. My readers may perhaps think that Philip had also fallen asleep and that his testimony is unreliable, but he has been trained to observe psychic phenomena and in any case there is other evidence – even more extraordinary – concerning transfiguration.

I have a Chinese guide called Chang Lung who is particularly helpful to me in my work as a clairvoyant and as a teacher. He is about forty, with a round face, and he usually wears a black hat and is very humorous. I have been told by my students that he sometimes transfigures me, as too does my German doctor helper. It is one thing perhaps to take on the characteristics of another woman, quite another to adopt the features of a Chinaman!

Of course one has to be extremely careful about trancing, which involves the conscious domination of one's own personality to let someone else step into one's body. I believe that my experience enables me only to give admission, so to speak, to someone in whom I can have confidence. In any case I would not allow a bad personality to take over. Since like attracts like, the possibility of being 'adopted' by an evil person is slight, but more important is the fact that trancing requires a willingness to be taken over. It is essential that someone should be present during a deep trance who understands that it can be dangerous. Coming out of such a state is not unlike recovering from an anaesthetic. I am always sleepy and cannot immediately function correctly, not at least until I have had a glass of water.

Deep trance takes a lot of energy from me, and partly because of this and partly because I can now usually achieve the same results without resorting to it, I have largely given it up. But there is no question about its efficacy in the right circumstances. My students at Belgrave Square used to tell me that, while I was in trance, it was quite usual for them to hear voices coming from all

141

directions, particularly behind my chair, and not just out of my mouth.

To revert to my Chinese guide, I know of course exactly what he looks like, but one day he came to me and said, 'You're going to get a surprise. Richard is going to draw a picture of me.' Richard was one of my students and at my next class I saw that he was in fact drawing something. 'It's Chang,' he told me. 'We've been seeing him quite clearly recently. It was meant to be a surprise.' It was an almost exact likeness of the Chang I knew!

Richard also gave me an oil painting, predominantly red in colour and Chinese in style. I became very fond of him and was faced with a difficult dilemma on his account. He was suddenly taken to hospital while I was away on tour, and he told the other members of the class who visited him that he would only get better when I returned. The doctors did not know for certain what was the matter with him. When in fact I saw him, I knew at once that he would die within two weeks and that he had cancer. He requested healing, which I gave him, and he said he felt much better. He then asked me when he would be leaving hospital.

I was in a fix. I could of course have lied to him or said I did not know, but I would never have told him he was about to die. I am not God, and anyway my knowledge might be wrong. I do not believe in giving people bad news except in certain circumstances as a warning, which if they heed will cancel the disaster. For example, a young man once walked into a meeting I was holding and I told him there was something wrong with his car. He denied it, saying he was quite sure I was wrong. I insisted that it was dangerous and that he should get rid of it. A week later it caught fire. My message so impressed the young man that he became very interested in the subject of psychic phenomena.

Alerting somebody to danger is all right, but not to

irreversible disaster or inevitable death. When Richard asked his question, I thought for a moment and replied, as casually as I could, 'Don't worry, you'll be out of here within fourteen days.' His sister telephoned me to say that he believed implicitly in what I had told him. And I was not wrong. Exactly fourteen days later he left the hospital to be buried. His painting and his drawing of Chang hang on my walls, so I can never forget him.

I am reminded of another painting, but first I must say something about Fanny Cradock, the famous cook and author. She and her husband Johnny will be remembered by millions who watched their marvellous cookery classes on television. I first met them at a party given by Fanny in publisher Peter Banda's house in Gerrards Cross. The Cradocks had long been interested in spiritualism, about which they were very well informed, and Johnny, as I soon discovered, has great healing power. They had however experienced so many false starts and disillusionments in their search for the truth that Fanny admits that she was prepared at first to avoid me like the plague. Yet as soon as she saw me she had a strong feeling she had known me in a previous existence, and we have been friends ever since. We got into conversation and Fanny says that, while she sat at my feet, I stroked her head. She had hated it when her father had done this, but did not mind my doing so.

The Cradocks have consulted me on many occasions since, but the first time stands out in their minds. I saw Johnny first and according to Fanny he came out as white as a sheet and told her that he had never had such clear evidence from a clairvoyant in his life. When I saw Fanny, I gave her the news that she would be moving to Ireland. She had no such intention at the time, but it was not long before I was proved right. I even predicted the month when she and Johnny would go. Later I visited her there and she told me she was unhappy. I said she would be moving to

Guernsey. I had a vivid picture of St Peter Port. 'You're not quite right,' she said, 'but you're not far off. We are thinking of going to the Channel Islands. In fact we're in the process of buying a house in Jersey.'

Philip and I happened to be on holiday soon afterwards in Jersey and, out of curiosity, we went to look at the house in question. The people living there kindly showed us around. 'Fanny will never live in this house,' I told Philip. A month later she telephoned to say that the deal had fallen through. Not long after that, the Cradocks moved to Guernsey.

I also told Fanny, who hitherto had mainly written cookery books, that she would write her family history and that, although sales would be slow to start with, the book would eventually prove very rewarding and would make a very successful film. In fact she had begun work on just such a project, but in fiction form and as part of a series. Not long afterwards she spoke to a publisher at a dinner party who asked to see the first book. One week later she received an offer to publish. The series did indeed start slowly but has gained momentum. If any film producer happens to read this book, he will be doing himself and Fanny a good turn by buying the film rights – and me too, because the best part of my prediction has yet to materialize!

When Fanny talks about me, she is always flattering. She says that I am the clairvoyant for whom she had been searching all her life. Recounting my clairvoyant exploits, she will say: 'I knew Doris was coming up with something important. That look came over her.' I asked Johnny to help me at an important healing meeting at the Commonwealth Institute in Kensington shortly after I had been named Spiritualist of the Year, and Fanny was on the platform – silent for once, but generally observing and recording – along with Michael Bentine, who chaired the meeting, and Philip who was also assisting with the healing. The hall was packed to capacity, and it was in fact my biggest healing meeting in England, second only to the audiences who came two years running to the Albert Hall where I was the clairvoyant for the Spiritualist Association of Great Britian. By and large, my audiences in Britain have been smaller than those in America, Australia, New Zealand and South Africa.

My readers will know by now that there are many different methods of healing. I heal by touch, by positive thought and by prayer; or in absence, just by thought and prayer. Clairvoyance undoubtedly plays its part, as for example when I am able to diagnose a problem that the patient does not know he has. For example, a man may say he has a bad back, and I may switch on to the fact that he has been having headaches as the result of a car accident. I healed my own grandson in 1973. This was my daughter's second child, Stuart, who was only three weeks old when Margaret rang me at Belgrave Square in a panic to say that the baby had been taken to hospital suffering from dehydration and that the doctors held out no hope for him. I was overcome by Margaret's faith in me and by the news that the child had been given only twelve hours to live.

I found it difficult to speak at first, while I considered the problem. Then I said, 'We'll start healing straight away. He'll be all right.' Beginning immediately I gave Stuart concentrated absent healing. He survived the night. I continued the healing at frequent intervals, and three weeks later he returned from hospital cured except for a hole in the heart caused by the dehydration. I do not wish to detract from the marvellous healing by the doctors and nurses at the hospital. I do not seek to take the place of the medical profession; I merely supplement their efforts. And who will ever know exactly what saved baby Stuart? All one can say with certainty is that the doctors initially despaired of

145

saving him. I have continued to give him healing ever since. I tune into him once a week regularly. The doctors now say that within a year the hole will have disappeared. Stuart is today a real charmer, strong and boisterous – the toughest in fact of all my grandchildren.

What most impressed Fanny about the big healing meeting were two cases. The first concerned a child of three or four who had never walked, and who many doctors had said would never walk. I agreed to attend to him after the meeting and sat him in a chair. After a few minutes' healing, Fanny records, I asked the child to stand, which to his parents' amazement he did. Then he took his mother's hand, his face radiant, and trotted happily with her across the hall and out of the door. Fanny was one of many people still in the hall who followed the child outside and who watched him walk across the car park to his parents' car.

The other case was that of a man who had been deaf for fifteen years. Fanny was intrigued when, after healing, I gradually moved away from him and lowered my voice, asking him questions. He answered every one, obviously having heard me clearly.

Almost exactly the same experience is recorded by Ken Attiwill, the husband of Evadne Price, the writer, television personality and astrologer. Although Australian, he joined the British Army as an anti-aircraft gunner during the last world war. He was later commissioned and won the Military Cross. He joined the ill-fated 18th Division in Singapore whose hopeless task was to try to stop the Japanese. It was during this terrible time that he was deafened by gunfire. Eventually he was captured in Java and spent three and a half years in a ghastly prison camp.

After the war, doctors and ear specialists told him that his condition was incurable. He wore a hearing aid, which he hated, and he longed for a miracle to restore him to his former state. He later developed a double cataract, and

146

could no longer see his lovely old farmhouse in Sussex. He decided to return to his native Australia. Evadne of course went with him and became his eyes and ears. The doctors however were more successful with his eyesight than his hearing, and when I was asked to give him healing, it was, thank God, only required for his deafness.

I met Ken because he was with Evadne when she chaired one of my big meetings in Sydney. According to his published report of the proceedings, I signalled him and took him by both wrists. He says that my hands were warm and vibrant and that power was transmitted to him. When he told me that he was deaf, I indicated two chairs that were facing each other. He sat on one of them while I stood, laid my hands on his head, moved them about his neck and ears and asked him questions about the origin and effect of his deafness. 'Her hands,' he wrote, 'felt tremendously strong. Yet her touch was more like a caress.' I told him to remove his glasses and hearing aid. Then I asked him to close his eyes and relax.

I removed my hands from his head, and he sat and waited. As if from a very far-off distance, he reports, he thought he heard a voice asking him a question. Was he 'hearing things', as they say?

Then he realized that it was my voice and that he really was hearing me.

'What is my name?' he heard.

'Doris,' he answered.

'Doris who?'

'Doris Collins.'

'Are you sure?'

'Yes, I'm sure.'

He heard another question, very faint but distinct. 'What is your name?'

'Ken Attiwill,' he said.

'Are you sure?'

147

He laughed at this. 'Yes, of that I am sure,' he replied.

A hand then touched his shoulder. It was Don Davis, who had been on the platform with me. 'Turn round,' he told Ken, 'and see where Doris is.'

Ken was amazed to see that I was on the platform about thirty yards away from him. 'You heard me,' I told him, 'because you answered my questions. . . You were deaf, but now you can hear.'

Ken Attiwill attests that his deafness was cured by my healing at the meeting. He regards it as a miracle and is extravagantly effusive in his praise of me. I am not embarrassed by this because if indeed there was a miracle, I was only its instrument.

I have written about this incident because it is so similar to the one independently witnessed by Fanny Cradock in which I used the same technique in healing a deaf man. Fanny also reminds me of something that happened while I was accompanying her to her new house in Ireland. She drove her Rolls, which contained eleven eight-foot laburnum trees, a carpet that the removal men had omitted to forward and furniture from her old home, as well as a mass of luggage. She put the car on the ferry, and when we arrived at crack of dawn at the customs in Cork, she was asked if she had anything to declare. 'Trees,' she boomed. I may say that I was wedged in the back seat under the trees and I was not apparently visible to the young customs officer, who then asked what was in the car boot. 'A carpet,' Fanny announced proudly. She was asked to open the boot, but it had stuck and she could not do so. She asked the officer to try, but he failed. 'Doris,' she suddenly yelled, 'you open the boot.' Whereupon, like the forest coming to Dunsinane, the trees moved and a large lady emerged from beneath them to the utter astonishment of the customs man. I rose with as much dignity as I could summon. 'This is ridiculous,' I said. 'Stand back!' And addressing the boot, I

148

commanded it to open at once. As if I had said 'Open Sesame', it sprang open at my touch.

I do not put this forward as an example of psychic power. It was more willpower on my part, born of frustration at the delay and my intense discomfort. Nor is this the incident to which Fanny was referring. That concerned a painting. During our journey we had stopped for lunch with John and Madeleine Stratton. They had owned the Bell House, the world-famous restaurant at Sutton Benger, and had now bought Ardwell's Restaurant, between Reading and Basingstoke, and a house nearby. Fanny had agreed to open the restaurant for her good friends. Following a magnificent meal, we were relaxing in the Strattons' new home when I admired a picture on the wall. It depicted a very pretty house with a millstream and a lake. It was in fact an old painting of the very house in which we were sitting.

Later I looked into the garden and saw monks walking across the lawn and disappearing into a wall. 'This must have been the site of the old monastery,' I said. Madeleine Stratton then said that she herself had seen monks one night who she thought had been chanting; and other people had claimed to have seen them, usually in the evening. There was a story that there had once been an underground passage from the site of the house to a big abbey.

When I looked again at the picture, I was convinced that a monstrous murder had been committed in the monastery grounds, but I did not like to say anything about this. On the journey Fanny told me, however, that when she had previously stayed the night in the house, she had woken up with a powerful thirst. There were very thick curtains on the windows and she could not find the light switch, so she had groped her way to the door to find the bathroom. The curtains in the bathroom were open, and the garden looked magical in the light of the almost full moon. When she returned to the bedroom, she pulled back the curtains for

149

another look at the garden. Then she yelled for her husband. To her horror she had, she told me, received a thought form of a hooded monk in a brown robe bending over a plank bridge to drown another monk in the mill-race.

Fortunately I knew that there was nothing for the Strattons to worry about. The evil that had taken place had long been expurgated, and theirs was a happy home.

For some reason – I think probably because another painting was involved – Fanny's experience put me in mind of something that happened many years earlier, when I was conducting my teaching circle in Ilford. One day after we had been meditating for about fifteen minutes, I asked my students, as was my habit, what they had seen or thought. One young man said he had seen a beautiful church, which he described. It was in a country village and had a lovely stained-glass window depicting the Last Supper. He had sat mentally in a back pew, in complete peace and not wanting to return in thought to this earth. Suddenly the door of the church opened and in walked the vicar with me at his side. As we entered, the organ started to play Handel's Largo.

It was at that moment that I summoned the class back to reality, much to this student's disappointment. He asked me whether I knew such a church, and I had to answer no.

Two weeks later a clergyman rang me from a village in Essex to ask if I would try to heal his wife. I had no car at the time and he lived some miles away in the country. I offered to visit them one Saturday afternoon if I could get transport. Almost immediately I received a telephone call from the Secretary of the spiritualist church of which I was President, who said, 'I've got a feeling you may need my services.' I knew he had a car and I asked him if he would drive me the following Saturday to see the clergyman's wife, which he was happy to do.

On arrival I got out of the car and an old gentleman in the spirit world came up to me and said, 'I brought you here. The vicar is my son. Will you tell him that I walk across the green with him from the rectory every Sunday morning and evening when he goes to take his services, and I'm very close to him today because I know he wants to help his wife to get better?'

I knocked at the door of the rectory and the vicar came and took me into his drawing-room where he told me that his wife had been going downhill for the past six months and that no one knew exactly what was wrong with her, except that her condition was presumably of nervous origin. She had fits of depression, trembling and breathlessness.

In the centre of the room, an attractive painting was standing on an easel. Sensing my interest, the vicar told me that his wife had painted it but that it remained unfinished because she had given up her hobby.

At that moment she entered and I asked if we could be alone, so that I could gain her confidence. She took me to another room and we talked for some time. I spoke about her painting and she said that she could not do it any more. 'Aren't you ever going to finish the one in the other room?' I enquired. 'One day I might,' she replied, 'but not now.'

'Would you paint one for me?' I said.

'No, I don't think I could,' she answered.

'You must,' I insisted. 'I'm going to give you a commission. I want to buy a picture and you're going to paint it.'

She became more enthusiastic and asked me what subject I was interested in. She had told me in the course of conversation that she was fond of Scotland, so I suggested a Scottish mountain scene. She said she would think about it, and I then gave her healing. Almost exactly a year later a beautiful watercolour reached me from the vicar's wife, which I interpreted as a sign that she had recovered from her illness.

After tea, I said goodbye to the lady, and the vicar offered to show me his church before I left. When we were alone, I told him about his father and the message I had been given. He seemed to accept it as perfectly natural. He opened the church door and we walked in together. Facing me was a stained-glass window depicting the Last Supper. The church was exactly as described by my young student a fortnight previously. But there was one thing missing. There was no music.

I thought we were on the point of leaving when the vicar suddenly said, 'We've got a new organ. Do let me show you.'

And he sat down at the organ and started playing Handel's Largo.

# Chapter Fifteen

In my late thirties I went to a local concert where I was impressed by a group of singers. I do not know about music being the food of love, but it certainly lightens the atmosphere at a religious meeting. A good singer can make a big difference to a religious service, and I tried wherever possible to have some sort of musical accompaniment at my public meetings.

The group in question were the Ivor Evans Singers, and I asked two of their members whether they would assist me at my next 'performance'. They asked me what I wanted them to sing, and I told them that they could choose what they wanted as long as it was not inappropriate. Following this, we arranged a practice session with a pianist, and I remember that one of the arias sung was 'One Fine Day' from *Madame Butterfly*. I myself joined in, I suppose because I loved the song and to jolly things along.

One of the professional singers surprised and delighted me by saying that I had a good voice, and asking whether I had ever thought of taking singing lessons and having my voice trained. I replied that I was far too busy with other things but I was persuaded reluctantly to talk to Ivor Evans himself. He was a distinguished baritone – I adored his rendering of 'The Song of the Flea' – who had been with the D'Oyly Carte Opera Company, and who now taught singing. He usually conducted the group and sometimes sang in it, along with his wife, who was a soprano.

I went along to see him, very hesitantly. 'Pity you've left it so long,' he said. 'You have the makings of a good voice, but you need to learn how to control it. Your breathing's all

153

wrong.' He told me that I was a natural contralto, and I thought of my Scottish grandmother who had sung professionally as a contralto. My voice however was a little too heavy and sombre. 'It needs more light in it,' he said. 'We've got to raise your pitch.' He then asked if I was willing to work hard if he undertook to teach me.

'I only want to sing for pleasure,' I said, somewhat rudely. 'I don't want to join your group.' But I decided to give it a try, and very grateful to Ivor Evans I am because he taught me how to control my voice not just as a singer but as a speaker too, so that I can today project my voice to the back of the average hall without the aid of a microphone. Hardly anybody ever complains that they cannot hear me.

After about six months we got to the point where my singing was in danger of taking me over. I felt I had to break away or my other work would suffer. The group needed another contralto to add weight to the choir, and there was pressure on me to join them. After much thought, I felt obliged to tell Mr Evans that my work was more important to me than my singing.

He looked at me for a moment and nodded. 'I don't want to lose you,' he said, 'but of course the decision is yours.' I wanted to tell him how grateful I was to him for his faith in me and what he had taught me, when he suddenly said, 'Will you at least sing in the festival with my singers at the Royal Albert Hall?'

I had to agree. In any case it was a great honour. It was only when I got home that I realized how improbable the whole thing was. If anybody had told me six months earlier that I would be entertaining the public as a singer, and in the Albert Hall at that, I would have thought they were mad.

The great day arrived, and I accepted what was happening as something perfectly natural, as though it occurred

154

every day of my life. I was in no way overawed by the occasion, or even nervous. After all, I was in the back row of the choir and hardly visible to the vast audience. I threw myself into the spirit of the occasion and decided to enjoy myself.

We had not been singing long when I heard the voice – not the voice of one of our group or one of the listeners in the hall, but a voice from far away and yet as clear and precise as could be. 'One day,' it told me, 'you will stand here alone!'

Stand here alone in the Royal Albert Hall? Surely the voice was mistaken. I had a good voice but I would never be a Kathleen Ferrier. I was not a good enough singer to be a solo artist. Suddenly I was frightened. Was the message designed to persuade me to give up my other work, which I regarded as more important to me, in favour of singing?

Paradoxically perhaps, it had the opposite effect. It forced me to consider the position and to make a choice. I decided to confirm my previously stated decision to give up singing. For once, one of my voices was wrong because I chose to make it so. Or at least so I thought. . .

On Remembrance Sunday, 11 November 1973, I stepped forward from the back of the platform at the Royal Albert Hall and stood alone for over an hour in front of a vast audience. My voice had been right after all. It was just that I had misinterpreted its message.

The occasion was the Remembrance Service organized by the Spiritualist Association of Great Britain. The evening was only slightly spoilt for me by the fact that my dear friend Peter Sellers, who was to have spoken at the meeting, could not get back from Cyprus, where he was filming, as he had intended. In his place, the meeting was addressed by the Reverend David Kennedy, the Church of Scotland minister whose book *A Venture in Immortality* gave evidence of survival from his wife in the spirit world. He made such a

155

powerful and interesting speech that it was easy to see why his book had been such a success.

It was my function – and that of Gordon Higginson, President of the Spiritualists' National Union – to demonstrate clairvoyance. Despite my great experience in this field, because this was the Royal Albert Hall and the occasion was so important to so many people in the audience, I was more nervous than I had been when I had been on the same stage as a singer. I do not remember a great deal about what I said or did that night, but fortunately the proceedings were reported in the press. What I do recall vividly is the sea of faces that confronted me when I began my demonstration. I felt terribly alone. Then I remembered the old voice, and this gave me confidence.

Surely nobody realized that evening as I stood there in a flowing green chiffon dress, carefully groomed and made up, that in the morning I had been on my knees repairing a loose pane in a glass door. Philip had advised me to relax. 'You should be resting,' he said, 'with such a big meeting to take.' But work is my relaxation, particularly gardening and needlework.

'Don't make it hard on yourself tonight,' Philip further advised me. 'The acoustics at the Albert Hall are notorious, so concentrate on the first few rows.' Unfortunately that is not always possible. I cannot control the messages I receive for people. They may be in the front row or in the very back row, or of course anywhere in between. I cannot call up the spirits at will. They communicate through me only if they choose, and while I admit that I almost inevitably receive messages for transmission, I have no way of arranging the location of the people for whom the messages are intended.

Thus one of the first persons I went to was a young man in a back row. 'You're from Australia,' I said, 'and the girl next to you is linked with you.'

'I only met her outside, and we got talking,' he told me.

'Well, she's going to mean something to you,' I insisted. The young man telephoned me two years later to remind me of the prediction and to say that they had just got married.

An American magazine once referred to me amusingly as an 'ESPecially gifted' woman. Writing in the magazine, *Probe the Unknown*, which explores paranormal phenomena, Robert Birchard referred to the change that he detected in me when I start to work on a public platform. He described me as taking command of the stage with an air of complete authority. 'Where she had seemed calm, almost placid,' he wrote, 'she now proceeded to surprise everyone . . . with a sparkling display of the often hidden, but fiery bit of prima donna that exists in every great professional, be it an opera star, a football quarter-back or a famous psychic.' I quote these words not to blow my own trumpet but because there is more than an element of truth in them. I am like an actor, a performer, when I work in public, and I project a strong personality, many people have told me. What they do not always realize is that the real me is a far less confident creature; my stage self takes me over.

The *Psychic News* reporter who covered the big Albert Hall meeting wrote that I showed no signs of nerves. I doubt if he would have so reported had he seen me a couple of hours earlier. He was intrigued by a mother who had a message for her child in the audience; the mother had died only four weeks previously. And he was amused by a woman from the spirit world who thanked a friend for having given her the bedsocks she had been wearing when she died. It is often these little, seemingly trivial messages that stay in the mind. Of course what may seem quite unimportant to me may be of the very greatest significance to the person who receives the message, as for example the child who appeared with a message for his mother; I distinctly heard him say, 'Hello, Mummy, I'm so glad to get to you.'

My part in this successful Remembrance Service resulted

157

in my being invited to participate in the following year's Service also. Famous healer Harry Edwards made a marvellous speech and it was again my job to demonstrate clairvoyance. Coral Polge and Gordon Higginson gave a double demonstration of psychic art and clairvoyance, and the Ebbw Vale Male Choir enchanted everybody with their beautiful singing.

I am told that the spirit communicators who manifested themselves through me showed unusually full awareness of the conditions and problems of the people in the audience for whom they had messages, but re-reading published reports of my part in the Service does not convince me that the quality of my participation was any different in the Albert Hall from what it would have been in less august circumstances. Indeed the very recounting of a series of similar messages – for in a sense all messages from the spirit world for living people are similar – tends to trivialize them; if I say to someone, 'His name is Will, not Bill' or 'He's not your Sid, he's Mary's Sid', that may verify the message for the recipient but it is not particularly interesting for an onlooker.

Only one item in the reports may be of wider interest. A young man who had served in the Royal Air Force came to me with a message for a lady in the audience who he said had been looking at a photograph of him the previous week. I went to a particular woman, sitting in the body of the hall, who immediately recognized the communicator as a boy she had known who had died at a young age, and she confirmed that she had indeed looked at his photograph only a few days earlier. I suddenly smelt a strong anaesthetic – apparently I reported this to the audience – and I told the woman that the young man had tried to help her eight or nine years ago when she was in hospital. She remembered the occasion well.

A camera crew recorded the second Remembrance Service in which I took part. This was for a German film. I have personal experience that the Germans are particularly interested in clairvoyance. Earlier in the same year I had received a telephone call from a German producer who was making a film about someone called Karl May. I had never heard of the producer or of Mr May, but that is because I am not German. Had I been I would surely have known that Karl May was a famous German author, long since dead, who wrote North American Indian stories. He had not been to America but wrote about places that he had never seen with a purported accuracy that defied normal reasoning.

The producer sought my help. 'We have heard about you,' he said, 'and we want you to authenticate certain circumstances of Karl May's life.' It must be highly unusual to employ a clairvoyant as a special adviser on a film. I was very intrigued and agreed to help if I could.

I went to Vienna and the producer said that he would like to sit with me to see what communication, if any, I received. He told me nothing about Karl May, beyond the fact that he was a writer of Westerns, and I had had no opportunity to make enquiries about him, even had I wished to do so; as I have said before, it is often better to know nothing about the people who communicate through me. 'I don't know if he will make his presence felt to me,' I said, 'but we can certainly experiment.'

So the two of us sat in my hotel room and waited. Very soon I became conscious of a man who told me that he had been brought up in a woodcutter's hut. He kept showing me an axe.

'That's Karl May,' the producer said excitedly. 'He was brought up in such a hut.'

The man then told me that he had been put in prison for stealing a watch.

'True,' the producer shouted.

'But I didn't steal it. I only borrowed it,' the spirit figure insisted. He then said that he had started writing in prison out of loneliness, using his imagination to invent characters and depict scenes. The producer was becoming more and more fascinated, for it was a fact that Karl May had begun to write while in gaol.

The dead writer then said something that even I thought was remarkable. He had had two wives, both of whom were clairvoyant, and when he was blocked in his writing – notably when he was stuck for realistic information about his characters or their background – he would sit with his wife who would go into trance and describe things to him that he put into his books. Could this have been the secret of their authenticity?

I was invited later to watch the shooting of the first scene of the film. It took place in a prison. I knew psychically that certain details were wrong and I was able to recommend changes, but I confess that I found film-making very boring, particularly since after four hours' work they had only made five minutes of the finished film! I wanted to return home in any case, and I felt that I had probably contributed as much as I possibly could to the film's success. I agreed however to the producer's request to give a séance in my hotel room for some of the principal people concerned with the film. ('Séance' was his word; it is not one I normally use; I much prefer 'sitting'.)

The occasion was photographed and reported in the local press. Among those present were Helmut Käutner, who played the part of Karl May in the film, and the two ladies who played his wives, Käthe Gold and Kristina Söderbaum. We had no communication with Karl May this time, but there was a visitor of a completely different kind. A very angry man came back from the spirit world and tried to put a collar round one of the actresses. The photographer did not see this but I did quite clearly.

'She's acting,' the man said, 'and I forbade it.' His voice was strong and menacing.

Later the actress in question told me that her husband had been a friend of Hitler. He had forbidden her to continue her acting career and had virtually kept her 'collared' while they were married; it was only after his death that she felt liberated. She had gone to America and become a successful photographer, and this film was her first acting part since her husband's proscription.

I can well understand sceptical readers of this book who find difficulty in believing all I write. Some may even think I am a fraud, or at the very least stupidly gullible. It is never easy to accept the truth of what one has not experienced personally and it is in any case less easy to prove survival after death than that the Battle of Hastings took place in 1066. There is concrete evidence to substantiate historical events, whereas much of the evidence that confirms paranormal phenomena is of a more abstract nature and does not always fit conveniently into people's preconceived ideas. If a witness in a court of law states that he has received a letter and produces the letter, its existence will be accepted; but if the same witness says that he has got a message from the spirit world, he may well be disbelieved. Everybody has experience of receiving letters, but not everybody receives messages from the departed.

It is for this reason that I have sought in this book only to include accounts of matters that can be vouched for by at least one person other than myself. There are many stories I could tell but that cannot be corroborated independently; I have therefore omitted them deliberately, preferring to rely on evidence, such as it is, that has been recorded or that other people will be able to confirm.

Literally hundreds of people have written to me over the years, reminding me of matters in which I have been involved; I am most grateful to them because I would not otherwise have felt able to include such matters in this book. One such example is worth quoting, not because it reveals anything very unusual from my point of view – although the writer obviously thought it most unusual – but because it is so well documented. My correspondent was a lady who had lost her son following an accident. She came to see me work at the Birmingham Civic Centre in August 1976.

According to her testimony, she knew instinctively that my second message, concerning a boy who had been killed in an accident, was intended for her. Although she had been to two previous spiritualist meetings, she had had no message from the boy, whose name was Robert, but he had apparently appeared to her sister-in-law who had woken up in the middle of the night and found the boy standing at the foot of her bed. He was smiling and said, 'Tell Mom not to worry.' Against her husband's advice, she had passed on the message.

Now the boy's mother was in my audience, convinced that I was referring to her Robert but too nervous to acknowledge her conviction. Instead two or three other people who thought that the message might be for them raised their hands, and I spoke to them, but I had to tell them that the message was not for them. At last a friend persuaded the lady in question to come forward, and as soon as I heard her voice I knew that she was the one.

She heard me say, 'Books, books, all around me,' and this put her in mind of the books that her son's college had returned; she was too heartbroken to look at them. I then told her that she carried two photographs of her son, but she said that I was referring to her husband; it was he who had two photographs in his wallet. He was in the lobby outside and I asked that he be brought into the hall.

This sort of mistake can easily be made by a clairvoyant. I presumably saw two pictures and misinterpreted their

162

exact significance. At a public meeting I have to work very quickly – there are always many people waiting to be attended to – and I have to obtain quick results. This involves taking some short cuts – I interpret messages in a sort of shorthand – and false interpretations are very possible; it is a wonder there are not far more. Sometimes however I am proved right when the receiver of the message thinks I am wrong.

I told this very same lady, for example, that Robert was one of three children. 'No,' she said, 'he is one of two.'

The message I was receiving referred positively to three children. Perhaps it was foolhardy of me but I responded immediately by saying, 'I will argue with you, dear, but not with them,' referring of course to people in the spirit world.

Imagine telling a woman she has had three children when she knows she has had two! But my seeming recklessness caused the lady to think, and she told me she had miscarried and lost a child. I suddenly saw that child, aged about six. It was standing next to Robert, and I put my hands out and indicated its approximate size. The lady had lost the baby in fact six years earlier, and she records that she was extremely impressed because for all I knew it had died before Robert was born. If I was at all impressed it was because the incident provided some possible evidence that an unborn baby can develop in the spirit world.

My next achievement was to name the lady's sister-in-law, Annie, and to say that the two women had lived together in the same house, both having an upstairs bedroom. She confirmed that this had been the case over twenty years ago. I then amazed her by saying that Robert had visited her sister-in-law recently.

I apparently then spoke of a garden shed that was used as

163

a workshop, and said that some of Robert's belongings were still there. Turning to her husband, I said, 'You went up there this morning, got as far as the door, changed your mind and walked back.' This was true. He had done just that, forgetting what he had gone for. 'Robert was with you then,' I told the husband. And I believe that this, more than anything, convinced the lady. The incident, she writes, was so unimportant and trivial that she had not given it a second thought, but if I were not receiving a message from Robert, how else could I possibly have known? Not another soul in the world except she and her husband knew about this minor domestic incident, which they would hardly have mentioned to anybody else.

'This is the first time Robert has got through to you,' I told the lady, 'and he is so excited.' Whereupon she records that I put my hands above my head and shook them. This was a mannerism of Robert's, and both she and her husband agreed that throughout the message I seemed to take on Robert's personality. For some reason I told her to get rid of a pair of Robert's sandals, in exactly the words and tone of voice, and with the same hand movements, that he would have employed.

Finally, before going to the next member of the audience, I called out 'Mike – Mick!' Robert had had a friend called Mick whom Robert's mother used wrongly to call Mike. 'It's Mick, Mom, Mick,' he would say. Now I had a message from Robert to Mick. It was very simple: 'Tell him I'm alive.'

The lady's account of my meeting in Birmingham concludes with a statement that she has never had another message since like that. There was no way in which I could have known what I told her and she would not have believed it possible had she not been the recipient. She ends with the following words:

'That my son Robert came through to us through Doris

164

that afternoon, there is no doubt, for who else could have known all those things? And both my husband and I blessed her for proving to us that after-life is a fact, and that once again I will hold my beloved son when my time is finished here.'

# Chapter Sixteen

My psychic, clairvoyant and healing faculties are combined
to some extent in whatever I do. Some people come to me as
a last resort when they are very ill, and of course it is my
healing that they require; but I cannot divorce healing from
my clairvoyance. As a medium I am often able to help
people, but the advice I give them comes from more than
one source. I say what comes into my mind, or, more
accurately perhaps, what is put into my mind. This is not
the same as commonsense because sometimes what I
advise seems to be the opposite of commonsense.

What I cannot do is make decisions for other people. I
can only help them to make their own decisions.

Over the years I have advised people from all walks of
life. Some think nothing of flying across the Atlantic for an
appointment, but I treat everyone alike. Rich or poor,
famous or unknown, people have similar problems and one
has to deal with them in the same way. Most people who
come my way have been recommended to do so or have
heard about me through word of mouth or as a result of my
public meetings. I do not deliberately advertise my existence. Some come out of curiosity rather than because they
have some great need.

The whole world of course is very curious about the
unknown, and I deal with the unknown. This, I believe, is
the explanation for the growing interest in the work of
psychics. Nowhere is this interest more evident than among
'show business' people, so many of whom have consulted
me in recent years. I have often seen my name in the
newspapers, not in my own right but by association with

some celebrity who has reported to a journalist what I said – which I would otherwise surely have forgotten!

With respect to Irving Berlin, show people are no different from any other people in essentials. But on second thoughts, he may have had a point. A lot of them are very psychic, and perhaps this enables them to interpret their roles. Just as I have to deal with two spheres of intelligence, the here and the beyond, so an actor has to develop an elasticity of mind to become many people.

Some of the richest and most successful people I know are the unhappiest – although this is not invariably the case. The problem with many performers is that they never seem satisfied with their achievements, and they need constant reassurance about the future. Was their last play or film or record really as good as the critics said? Had they really made it, and if so would they lose it? Their basic pessimism is, I suppose, endemic in a business where you are only as good as your last success.

This helps to explain why so many celebrities have sought my advice and help, but I can only write about those who have either given me permission or else, like Peter Sellers, have themselves publicized the fact that they have consulted me. As I have said before, all sitters come alike to me, and I am not sure that I had ever met a film or television star until I was demonstrating clairvoyance one evening in the celebrated Ambassador Hotel in Los Angeles.

I had asked a group of musicians to play and sing while the audience was assembling. When the room filled, the musicians left the stage without taking their instruments and equipment. I need to walk up and down while I am working and could not do so for the clutter. So I requested a good-looking man in the front row to help me clear the platform. He was wearing jeans and an open-necked shirt and I selected him because he looked tall and strong.

167

'Certainly, ma'am,' he said willingly, and within a very short time I was able to work.

There was a reception for me afterwards in a room upstairs, and the first person to come forward and shake my hand when I arrived was the man who had helped me earlier. He introduced himself as Clint Walker, whom millions of people will know as Cheyenne. He later invited me to dinner at his home, where I met his lovely French wife who had been a singer. We had a delightful evening during which he played a guitar and sang a number of songs of a spiritual nature which he had composed himself. He gave me a book of paintings of American Indians by Frank McCarthy which both he and his wife signed and which I very much treasure.

During the evening, he asked me to give him healing, which I gladly did. He told me that healing had saved his life and that that was why he was so interested in my work. While he was filming, a ski pole had penetrated his chest, just missing his heart. He had lain in hospital, near to death, for several weeks and felt that the healing he had received, in addition to the expert medical attention, had made the vital difference. He would do anything, he told me, to further what he called the science of spiritual healing.

I have given healing to many other show-business personalities. When Frankie Howerd broke his pelvis, he telephoned me, full of woe, asking for healing which I gave him by absent thought. 'You'll soon be better,' I told him. 'You'll be in London in just over a week.' 'Don't be bloody silly,' he said, 'I've broken my pelvis.' What I did not tell him was that he would be in hospital in London within the week – which was certainly true, because I went to visit him there. He made an almost miraculous recovery.

There are so many similar stories I could relate, but one is very much like another. Anthea Redfern, for instance, when she was married to Bruce Forsyth, came to me for help because she believed she could not have children. I told her that she would give birth to a child but I also said I had found great comfort in adopting a child, so I advised her in any case to follow my example, and she did eventually adopt a baby girl. But it was no surprise to me when a few months afterwards she gave birth to a child, another daughter, as I had predicted.

My dear friend Michael Bentine, himself an authority on the paranormal, has frequently asked me to help him and his family. I forecast even before he wrote it that his book *The Door Marked Summer* would be on the bestseller lists. He is one of my greatest supporters and never fails to sing my praises to anyone interested in the fields in which I work. It is Michael who encouraged me to write this book. He asked me to see Pete Murray soon after Pete's son had died in very tragic circumstances. I hesitate to mention this matter but it was so widely reported in the press that I feel I should do so. The young man came back and spoke through me to his father. Apparently what he said was so amazingly accurate that it brought great comfort to Pete.

Among celebrities, it is not only show people who take an interest in my work. If I may just pick one name, I will refer to the late Sir Douglas Bader, the air ace who lost his legs in an air accident and whose courage was a shining example to everyone. Whenever possible, I give my services to the Cheshire Homes, who hold a fête once a year. They treat me as a sort of resident clairvoyant for the day. It is hard work but the patients love it, as do their families and friends, so it is also rewarding. On one such occasion – it was the first time I had met him – Douglas Bader opened the proceedings and, referring to me, jokingly said, 'I'm going to be the first in.' He was indeed my first sitter at the fête that year.

I do not know whether he believed when he went in, but

he certainly did when he came out, as he told people subsequently. I have seen reports in the press that he was convinced about life after death, presumably having known so many young pilots who had died before their normal time.

The following story has been printed on more than one occasion, and Bader told it to millions on the Parkinson Show, and I know that it provided him with what he regarded as substantial evidence of my bona fides. Apparently he had gone to see his old friend Henry Longhurst, the golfer, in hospital. This was shortly before Longhurst's death. Longhurst had indicated that it would not be long, as he put it, before he found out whether the grass was greener on the other side.

One of the messages I received for Bader was from a man named Henry. 'Does the name mean anything to you?' I asked. 'He says that the grass *is* greener.'

Thereafter Douglas Bader kept contact with me and often sought my advice. On Friday, 3 September 1982 he telephoned me personally, saying, 'I want to consult you professionally.' I could tell that he had a very urgent need to see me but I was just about to leave for a committee meeting of my healing association. I told him that I would telephone him that evening if I returned early enough; otherwise I would contact him the following morning.

In fact I tried to reach him on the Saturday morning but he had already left for London where he was planning to dine that evening with an old friend. 'I'll ring him tomorrow morning,' I said, 'to make an appointment to see him on Monday.' 'No, that's a bad time,' I was told. 'He always plays golf on Sunday morning, so leave it till the afternoon.'

Douglas Bader was taken ill after dinner on the Saturday night and died early on the Sunday morning. I felt instinctively that he must have known he was going to die and that that was why he had wanted to see me, and this impression

170

was confirmed when Lady Bader, his widow, was reported in a newspaper as having said: 'I think he made the last appointment because he realized the end was near.'

It is no secret that Peter Sellers was closely concerned with the psychic world, and I was by no means the first psychic he had consulted; but for almost the last ten years of his life I must have been important to him because we were in constant touch.

I was in my early fifties and Peter in his middle forties when we first met. He had made an appointment to see me under an assumed name. This is not uncommon in my experience. Perhaps people think that if I know who they are, I will check up on them, thereby devaluing what I tell them. I have never in fact checked up on anybody in my life; I am just not interested and in any case I am too busy. People seem to think that their names are important, but they are not to me. I do not go by reputation.

We met at the flat of a friend of mine in London. Peter entered quickly and I did not recognize him, but during the sitting it became obvious to me who he was from the evidence I was receiving. In particular his mother, with whom he was very close, came through. She said something very curious: 'Will you tell my son I'm going to put his name in the press at every opportunity?'

Peter later told me that he had been going through a bad patch at the time – at least he thought so – and in fact from that time on his name never seemed to be out of the newspapers, not always in the happiest of circumstances. Perhaps his mother believed that all publicity is good publicity.

He was married at the time to his third wife, Miranda, and I had to tell him that the marriage would not last. No doubt many people could have made that sort of prediction to a man like Peter Sellers, but my information came to me clairvoyantly of course. It was not long afterwards that he

171

met Liza Minnelli. By then Peter and I had become firm friends and I saw him frequently. I had met him after my divorce from Richard Collins and I married Philip in the same year that Peter met Liza.

Fortunately Peter approved of Philip, but until he saw him face to face he was very wary. 'For God's sake,' he insisted, 'let me see him. Don't do anything stupid.' (Look who's talking, was the thought that went through my mind at the time!) Anyway, after our marriage he asked Philip and me to go to his mews house in Belgravia to receive an Indian blessing from him. He was very much into Indian cults and had a guru in New York. We were obliged to crouch on the floor for a full thirty minutes, until I thought my knees would give way, while all three of us held hands and Peter chanted in some foreign tongue. On a later occasion I received a telegram from him which contained the following words, similar to those he sang to us at the little ceremony: SATCHITANANDA EXISTENCE KNOWLEDGE BLISS HARE OM HARE KRISHNA SHANTI SHANTI SHANTI.

The interlude with Liza Minnelli did not last long, but I knew about it from the start. I do not think Peter believed me when I told him that his marriage to Miranda would end, but he telephoned one day to tell me that he was in love with Liza. 'You're right, Doris,' he said. 'I've met the girl of my dreams. She's absolutely fantastic.'

He brought her to see me while I was in hospital recovering from surgery. They had announced their engagement although Peter was still married. Liza told me that she was in love with Peter but was actually expected to marry a well-known American actor. She asked me whether she should do so, and I remember saying no. Peter and Liza held hands all the time and gazed into each other's eyes, but it was not long afterwards that he rang me to say that she had left him.

This did not surprise me. I had already told Philip that their alliance would end as suddenly as it had started. Liza is a fantastic, dynamic personality; Peter said she had hypnotized him with her tremendous power. Peter was many people – sometimes arrogant and difficult, sometimes a little boy who needed a mother – and I knew it could not work.

I later told Peter that he would marry for a fourth time. 'Rubbish,' he said. 'I've had enough,' and then he told me about a girl who had walked out of his life before his first marriage and whom he had never been able to find. I knew that she must have meant something very special to him. I think what impressed him more than my forecasts about his marital status was my prediction that he would make three films in one year. He said that was impossible, but when it came to pass he started to consult me very frequently.

What a natural actor he was. He confessed to me that he lived the part he was playing at the time. It took over his personality. The problem was that he could turn on a performance at a second's notice, as one might switch on a light. I was with him on one occasion when a lady telephoned who had obviously been an interlude in his life and who thought that she still remained important to him; he cannot have told her that their affair was over. Peter gave a ludicrously funny double performance, speaking in one voice to her and in another to me with his hand over the mouthpiece.

She told him that she had been delayed. 'Oh, darling,' he said, 'I'm so sorry. Hurry up; you know how much I miss you.' Turning to me, 'My God,' he said, 'I hope she never gets here.'

She said she would arrive as soon as possible. 'I can't wait, darling,' he told her. 'Catch the next plane over.' Then to me, 'I hope she misses it, she's such a pain.'

Both speeches were made with total conviction. I felt

173

sorry for the lady because Peter was being two people. This was relatively uncomplicated for him because he could be several people, and this doubtless explains why there have been so many conflicting reports about his character and his behaviour. He was wonderful as a friend, but he must have been very difficult to live with.

He was famous for his telegrams, often pages long. I was one of many people who would receive an angry message, followed not long after by a message of apology. It is somewhat disconcerting to be torn to pieces at one moment and an hour later to be asked: 'Please forgive. All is well.'

Although Peter did not smoke and drank very little, at least in my presence, he went to extremes in many other ways. Could that have had anything to do with his weak heart? He was very health-conscious and in fact for most of the time I knew him he was on a health kick. He used to take me to Chinese restaurants and eat dried seaweed. So I saw mostly the moderate Peter Sellers. But I also saw the way in which he went from one extreme to another, and back again. What I did see very clearly was his great remorse that often followed bouts of bad or extravagant behaviour. It was remorse akin to atonement which led him to seek spiritual knowledge from eastern gurus. Of that I am sure. His inner personality, which I was privileged to know, had a strong spirituality.

Sometimes when I arrived he would come to the door with a tape recorder in case I was a reporter. He wanted his words recorded so that he could not be misinterpreted. I think however that misinterpretation in his case was sometimes accidental. Being so many people in one, he could be all things to all men, and I can easily credit two completely different versions of a story about him. For my part, I prefer to remember the good in his complex character.

I did not see Peter after his fourth marriage because he and his wife, Lynne Frederick, lived mostly in Switzerland

and the United States. He kept in touch with me however and after his death Lynne told me that he had spoken to her about me. I never met her while Peter was alive and it was at Peter's funeral that Lynne asked Michael Bentine how she could find me. It happened that the Bentines had invited Philip and me to lunch the following Saturday, so they asked Lynne to come along too. I had deliberately arrived early so that I could talk to her before lunch. It was a very bright and sunny day and everyone except Lynne and me went into the garden.

She struck me as a very sad and tired girl. No sooner were we alone than Peter contacted us, giving Lynne some very personal information that only the two of them could have known. I was surprised when later a full report of Peter's messages appeared in the daily newspapers, but I suppose that everything concerning him was always news. Peter admitted that he had never been an easy man to live with and said that Lynne had at one time contemplated leaving him; but he had loved her and needed her and would not willingly have let her go. He added that he had married her with his mother's wedding ring, and that she was the only woman to whom he had ever given it. He also revealed the terms of his will.

Lynne asked if she might put a question to Peter. 'Ask, and we'll try to get an answer,' I said.

'Peter,' she then said, as if testing him, 'it's soon going to be your birthday. Could you tell me what I'm going to do on your birthday as a special present to you?'

'Yes, I can,' came the reply. 'You're going to give me a wonderful send-off, because this morning you arranged a memorial service for me at St Martin-in-the-Fields.'

I understand that the arrangements for the service on Peter's birthday, 8 September, had been completed only a couple of hours earlier, and Lynne had had no opportunity to mention the matter. She told a reporter that the message

175

had given her great peace of mind and that she had had her first good night's sleep that Saturday night since Peter had been taken ill. According to this same reporter, she said: 'I am totally convinced that it was Peter we made contact with.'

Philip and I received invitations to the memorial service and Michael Bentine hired a limousine for the occasion and arranged to collect us. He was of course going with his wife, Clementina. But unexpectedly the Prince of Wales, who had hoped to attend, was unable to do so and asked Michael to represent him. Protocol required that Michael arrive in the royal car, and furthermore the ceremony could not begin without him! The limousine therefore drove us first to Buckingham Palace, where we dropped Michael, and then to the church, where we were seated in the third row. I noticed Michael Caine almost directly in front of me and the Beverley Sisters right behind. Lord Olivier and Spike Milligan were in the same row, and Sir John Gielgud nearly fell over my feet as he negotiated his way past me. Everywhere one looked, there were show-business celebrities of every type, as well as famous people from other walks of life.

Sizing me up after the service, Harry Secombe, himself no lightweight, cheerfully boomed: 'They'll want a bloody big hole to put you and me in, Doris, when we go.' In more serious vein, he had earlier sung a hymn, and most movingly too. Lord Snowdon had read the 23rd Psalm and David Niven had given a most wonderful address, in which he happened to refer to Peter's apparent dislike of writing letters but his characteristic use of sometimes very lengthy telegrams. 'I'm sure,' he said, 'many of us have been in receipt of a cryptic telegram, followed immediately by another telegram cancelling the nasty remarks.' I was of course among their number. 'He must,' David Niven continued, 'have supported the Post Office's revenue.'

As he said this I saw Peter appear at Niven's side, together with his mother and another lady. And then I heard him say, 'So telegrams are my epitaph, are they?'

Philip had to return to his office after the service, so Clementina Bentine and I returned to Buckingham Palace to collect Michael. We were invited in for refreshments by the Prince's Private Secretary and Treasurer. He asked questions about the ceremony and also about my work, saying that he was very interested in the subject of healing, having himself received healing through an army colleague.

That evening Lynne telephoned to ask how I felt the service had gone. I told her that I had seen Peter, and she said she had sensed his presence. I also mentioned his mother and the lady I had not recognized. From my description Lynne identified her as Peter's favourite aunt, his mother's sister.

Some weeks later I received from Lynne a pair of spectacles that Peter regularly wore. They are a delightful reminder of a man who in some ways was my greatest publicity agent – a complex character who needed continual reassurance and who for a number of years was a very dear friend.

## Chapter Seventeen

I have tried in writing this book to refer only to happenings that are capable of verification, at least in the sense that there is an independent witness to everything I have recorded. As far as my own personal experiences are concerned, I realize that the reader has to some extent to take me on trust and that some of the things I recount are hard for some people to believe. Except for matters of record, I have attempted therefore only to mention incidents that I discussed at the time with other people who will, if necessary, be able to confirm that I have not invented them for the purpose of my book.

There are many occurrences that appear strange because they are not experienced on a regular basis by all and sundry; but that is not to say that they cannot and do not happen. Perhaps because I am psychic I either attract the unusual or am more receptive to it. Maybe because I have sat to develop physical mediumship, I recognize the unusual for what it is – a natural phenomenon – instead of regarding it as a figment of imagination or even delusion. It can of course be the latter, but in the absence of evidence of insanity on the part of the person claiming to have experienced it, I prefer to accept the reality of its existence.

In 1980 I went to Finland to fulfil a series of public and private engagements which had been arranged for me and which took me all over the country, from Helsinki to Lapland and the border with the Soviet Union. I would have cancelled the trip, on the advice of my doctor, had extensive plans not already been made, because I had developed an ulcer on my right leg, which was in plaster, and I was walking at the time with the aid of two sticks. I explained the problem to my hosts and told them that they would have to look after me, which they agreed to do.

It was in Rovaniemi, on the Arctic Circle, that I had a very extraordinary experience. We flew there in the early morning, there being only one flight a day from the capital, and the snow was four-foot thick on the ground. I was met by the man who was to be my interpreter and with whom I was to stay. We drove by car to his lovely modern flat, where I was introduced to the lady of the house who did not speak a word of English. There was a little shop opposite my bedroom window and I was highly amused by watching the women do their shopping. They arrived with what looked like rocking chairs on skis, and it was very funny to see old ladies who could hardly walk place their purchases on the chairs, mount the skis at the back of the chairs and scoot down the hill as if the Devil were behind them. It was like looking at dog sledges without the dogs, but I am sure the contraptions were very practical.

I had risen early to catch the plane and was not of course in the best of health, so I told my host that I wanted a good rest before the evening, when I had a public meeting to deal with. My room was a double one with a large bed. I removed my dress, lay on the bed and covered myself with a blanket. I thought that if I actually got into bed, I might not want to get up later. I shut my eyes to rest them.

I had hardly made myself comfortable, and I was certainly not asleep or even dozing, when I heard chattering all around me. There were people in the room. Perhaps, thinking I was asleep, they had come to inspect the strange creature in their midst from England. Cautiously, out of politeness rather than fear, I opened one eye slightly and I was right: there were people in the room, but they

179

were little people, no higher than the bed. They climbed up and pushed pillows behind my back, tucking me inside the blanket like a child.

I felt like Gulliver but I knew their intention was to look after me. Could they have been Lapps, I wondered? I had heard that Lapps were not very tall but these people were tiny, like midgets. As suddenly as they had come, they went. The chattering ceased and there was total silence. I drifted off to sleep.

I woke up at about three o'clock in the afternoon. Only the lady was in the house but I could not question her. So I washed, dressed and started preparing for the evening meeting while I awaited the return of my interpreter. When I told him what had happened and asked him who the little people were, he looked at me nonplussed. He spoke to my hostess and then said quite simply that she had told him that nobody had been in the flat. There was something strange in his expression and I decided not to pursue the matter because they obviously did not seem to know what I was talking about.

The meeting was a great success and the following day I travelled to Tampere, where I met the man who was to return with me to Helsinki and act as interpreter for three days. He had taught at London University and spoke impeccable English but he said he thought he might find his job difficult since he knew nothing about my work. I told him not to worry, and to reassure him I also told him a great deal about himself, which appeared to amaze him. We went for a walk in the countryside the following day, and I related my experience in Rovaniemi. I expected him to laugh when I spoke of the little people, and his reaction surprised me. 'Yes,' he said, 'I fully understand.'

'You believe what I've told you?' I asked.

'Of course I do,' was his reply. 'You are in the land of the trolls.'

180

I am not sure that I knew at the time what a troll was. I had some vague idea that it was the name given to the toy mascots that some people hang in the windows of their cars, and I knew nothing of the friendly but impish dwarfs of Scandinavian mythology.

'You are in the land of the spirit people,' my informant continued, and he told me that when he went fishing for two or three days, he never locked his car as he did in town. He would talk to the trolls and seek their protection for the car. He himself believed that they existed in the mountains, and he told me about the place nicknamed Father Christmas Mountain which many people in the area believe is where the trolls live. The Lapps, he said, certainly believe in the little people.

Even had I not seen them I would have had no difficulty in accepting their reality. As a child I was always very drawn to the garden and particularly to plants; in fact I still am. I would play in the garden for hours and I regularly saw little creatures, no more than two or three inches high, on the branches of trees. They were not much bigger than long butterflies and I used to talk to them, thinking they were fairies. When I first told my mother, she entered into the spirit of things by pointing and saying, 'That's where Tom Thumb lives,' and I used to say that I was going into the garden to see Tom Thumb. So I would probably not have found it too difficult to believe in the trolls if someone else had told me about them and I had not seen them myself. My fairies may have been a product of my childish imagination, although I do not for a moment think so; but in any case the fact that I have not seen them since I was a child does not necessarily mean that they do not exist. Myth is often based on truth.

It may be thought that although I knew nothing about the trolls before my experience with them, they came into my mind psychically and that I imagined the whole epi-

181

sode. Being sensitive to atmosphere and being in a place where their existence was legendary, they might well have come into my mind. This of course is true, but I can only say that I am convinced that the trolls were actually there in my room and that I both saw and heard them.

People who know me realize that I am not easily taken in by nonsense and charlatanry and that I have my feet very firmly on the ground. They at least will vouch for my honesty. Yet I realize that I am testing everybody's credulity when I report the following event that also happened in Finland. I am however a hundred per cent certain that it happened.

I spent the last night of my Finnish visit in the Helsinki flat of the President of the country's psychic association. The flat was high up and the big picture window afforded an exciting view of the city and its glittering lights. I rarely draw bedroom curtains and the room in which I slept was therefore never dark. It was in fact a bed-sitting room that my hostess used also an an office. A long narrow table, full of photographs and other objects, stood between the bed and the window.

I had no sooner got into bed and was beginning to doze off when something almost incredible happened, so quickly that I had no time to analyse it. I was suddenly lifted clean in the air and over the table in the direction of the window! Although I had heard of levitation, such a thing had never happened to me before, and my first thought was that I was going clean through the window to my death. But no, I was deposited safely on the floor beneath the window, although at first I did not know where I was. My concern then was for my bad leg, but by some miracle I had only stubbed the big toe on my good leg. It was as if I had fallen on a bed of air.

When I realized what had occurred, I crawled to the door, got up and switched on the light. Then I saw that not only had I been propelled through the room but all the bedclothes, including the pillows and even the mattress, had been thrown eight feet or so off the bed and over the table. They were lying on the floor near where I had landed. What was quite amazing, considering my weight alone, was that not one single object on the table had been in any way disturbed.

I wish now that I had woken the other people in the house so that they could have seen with their own eyes what had happened to the mattress and the bedclothes, and been able therefore to confirm that I had not been dreaming the incident. But partly because I did not like to disturb them late at night and partly because I was bewildered by my experience, I did not do so. I can remember giggling to myself and thinking what a strange country Finland was: first I had been tucked up in bed by the trolls and then thrown out of bed by some unknown force.

Eventually I restored the mattress to its rightful place, remade the bed and fell asleep. At breakfast in the morning I apologized if I had made a noise in the night, and explained what had happened. My hostess told me that they had heard a sound like a loud bang which had caused them to jump out of bed and rush to my room. They had listened at the door but all was quiet and they had not wanted to bother me therefore. 'It was quiet,' I said, 'because I was so startled, I just had to lie on the floor to recover.'

At least there was independent evidence of a commotion in my room, and even more important was that my host and hostess believed me, although they described the happening as amazing. The lady actually offered a possible explanation. 'We had someone in our society,' she told me, 'who opposed your coming and tried to stop it. We've since dismissed this man.' One of the people who saw me off to England at the airport later that morning was a musician who was active in Finnish psychic circles. He too said something similar. 'Do you remember your telling me about the trolls tucking you in?' he asked. 'Well, they were protecting you because they knew someone was going to try to hurt you.' And it did seem at one time as if things were conspiring to stop me working effectively. Was it too fanciful to think that my bad leg may have been caused by evil thought or behaviour on the part of someone who wished me to fail?

I would hardly expect anybody to describe me as light as a feather, but I must have risen like a feather when I was levitated. I have no other personal experience of that particular phenomenon, but I have seen manifestations of other physical occurrences, including materialization and dematerialization. Plants, flowers and small objects have often moved, as if by themselves, from room to room in my house. I sometimes wonder whether this is their means of attracting attention. I once lost my engagement ring, a two-stone diamond given to me by my first husband. It was not loose and I had worn it on the same finger as I had my wedding ring for three or four years until one day it disappeared from my finger, and I never found it. I had put it on just before going into Ilford with Brian, who was in his pushchair. We had only gone four or five yards from the house when I realized that the ring was not on my finger. I was very worried and, although I knew I had not dropped it, I searched the house thoroughly. Of course the loss of an object is very rarely the result of dematerialization – there are many more obvious explanations for losing something – but my experience told me that this was no ordinary disappearance.

The incident made quite an impression on me at the time and I discussed it with several knowledgeable people in the psychic world. They found no difficulty in believing that mine was no conventional loss, and I was told that

184

sometimes things are dematerialized because someone has greater need of the object than the owner! I did not then know that the day would come when the ring would mean nothing to me anyway following my divorce.

On the same subject, Don Davis and his wife Mary from Australia were staying with Philip and me when Don lost his wallet. It contained a considerable sum of money, credit cards, travellers cheques and notes he had made during his visit to England. He had returned home to us late the previous night after dining and visiting the theatre. He was sure he had had the wallet after dinner but could not find it the following morning. 'What did you pay the taxi with?' I asked. 'Silver,' he replied, 'from my pocket. I didn't get my wallet out at all.'

He was clearly under the impression that the wallet was somewhere in the house, so we searched the place from top to bottom in a manner that would have done credit to Scotland Yard, but we did not find it. Don and Mary had to leave for a luncheon appointment in town and while they were out I again searched the house, feeling in some way responsible since the loss had occurred under my roof, although I knew that I was wasting my time.

The wallet was missed on a Saturday and I spent an unhappy weekend as a result. On the Monday Don had a number of engagements to keep and in case he did not have time to go to his bank, I pressed on him £100 which I had in the house. He thanked me and said that he would return it that evening if he got to the bank or else the following day. He went upstairs with the money in his hand and asked Mary to lend him her wallet in which to put the banknotes.

Downstairs we suddenly heard Don's excited shout: 'Doris, Philip, quick, quick, come up!' Philip and I rushed upstairs as fast as we could. Don and Mary were in their bedroom and Don was holding *two* wallets in his left hand! Both Philip and I saw this quite clearly. Mary said that

Don had been standing at the foot of the bed with my £100 in his right hand and her wallet in his left; when fantastically his own wallet appeared in the same hand. Had Don been a practical joker and a magician to boot, I might have found a 'logical' explanation for the wallet's reappearance, although he would not have let us suffer of course over the weekend; but he was neither of these things, and I am convinced that this was a simple case of materialization.

I was conscious, as I have explained, of strong psychic forces in Finland, and particularly in Lapland. A year following my visit to that country I made my first trip to Israel. This time however I was on a short sightseeing holiday, arranged by an American friend whom I had helped at a time when he had great need. I went out just before Christmas of 1981 and was so impressed by what I saw that I returned again towards the end of 1982. It was while visiting the Dead Sea that I became convinced that oil would be discovered in Israel, and I told this to the Mayor of Jerusalem to whom I was privileged to be introduced. He said that asphalt tar, a derivative of oil, had in fact been discovered floating on the Dead Sea, and that if oil were there in any quantity, it would dramatically affect his country's economic situation. I suggested to him an area that I felt might usefully be investigated.

The real interest to me however of my visit to Israel was in seeing Masada, where I had one of the most extraordinary experiences of my life. Masada, Herod's amazing fortress in the Judaean Desert one mile west of the Dead Sea, was the scene of a mass suicide by the Jewish Zealots to avoid capture by the Romans nearly two thousand years ago.

I went there with a friend in the company of a professional guide, who drove the car. It was a very hot day and I sat in front with the driver. I am sure that the guide knew nothing about me and that, as far as he was concerned, I

186

was just another tourist, but he suddenly said to me without any preliminary broaching of the subject, 'You're a psychic, aren't you?'

'How do you know that?' I asked, to which he replied, 'We Jews can be very psychic too. I just felt it.'

On arrival, we went up in a cable-car to the first plateau and then made the tiring, and to me slightly perilous, climb up the stone steps to the top. My friend, who had been there before, elected to sunbathe on the grass while I set off with the guide to investigate Herod's palace. I was shown all round, and then we sat down for a rest at a point on the eastern wall. I started to talk to the guide about himself. I told him that he had recently married and that his wife had just had a child, and I spoke about his plans for the future. He indicated that I was correct in everything I had said about him. 'There, you see,' he added in triumph, 'I knew what you were.'

It was then that he told me that he did not normally bring tourists to this particular spot, which he regarded as a very private place. 'Would you look over the wall,' he requested, 'and tell me what you see?'

I did so. I looked down and saw what looked like an encampment for an ancient battle. There were Roman soldiers everywhere and chariots. I also heard a great tumult. With astonishment I told the guide about this amazing scene; it was almost as if I were part of it. 'I'm glad you see it,' he said, 'because I do every time I come here.'

As he spoke I had a tremendous urge to throw myself over the top. Something heavy in my hands seemed to be impelling me. So strong was the feeling that I had to step back. I told the guide about this. 'Yes,' he said, 'you probably did just that.' I think he meant throw myself over the top. 'Do you know the history of Masada?' he asked.

187

'No,' I had to confess, 'I don't know anything about it.'

'Well,' he went on, 'I brought you to this spot because I was sure you would feel what I feel when I come here.'

As I walked about the ruins I had a very strong feeling that I had been there before. 'Yes,' my companion said when I told him, 'I recognized that the moment you got in the car. You have been here before. You were Jewish in a previous incarnation.' Then he told me how the Jewish defenders had committed suicide rather than surrender to the Roman soldiers.

My second visit to Israel, at the end of 1982, was part of a tour organized by the President of the Greater World Spiritualist Association. Following the happy time I had had on my first visit, I was quick to accept an invitation to join a group of about a hundred spiritualists and their friends. This time Philip accompanied me, and he described it as one of the best holidays of his life.

We started off with a young man as tour guide but after the first two days a young girl from Rio de Janeiro took over; although she was of course Brazilian, she had lived for some time in Israel. Gordon Higginson, who was on the tour, told me that this young lady had asked for a sitting with me. Why me, I wondered, when I was only one of many mediums in the party? 'Well,' Gordon said, 'she's asked me to ask you.' I had not intended to work on the holiday but I spoke to her about her request. She had heard about me from some South African people and, seeing my name on the list, had hoped that I might help her. She also told me that she sat in a circle in Israel to develop mediumship, so I realized that we could not have had a more understanding guide, and I believe that she told us things that were not always to be found in the guide books.

Part of the tour took in Masada but I was reluctant to go there again. The place had had a most powerful effect on

188

me the year before; in fact I do not think I have ever been more affected by a place. My first visit to the Highlands of Scotland had haunted me for a time and I remember being strangely moved when I first went to California; I felt strongly that I had lived there before, although I could not begin to say when or in what circumstances. But Masada was something different. My friendly guide had told me last year that I had been Jewish in a previous incarnation; what he did not know was that I had often thought this myself. Indeed I actually had a sort of conviction that I had lived in Palestine, or somewhere in what we now call the Middle East, at the same time as Jesus, and my experience at Masada had served to confirm this belief.

Whatever the truth about possible previous existences, I would not have returned to Masada had I been alone, but Philip was most upset when I tried to cry off, so I relented. As soon as I got up there again, I had the same strange experience as though my present life was unreal and I was walking in another world. In fact I felt physically ill, causing Philip to remark how pale I had gone, but I went everywhere with the group.

Eventually the guide too asked if I were feeling ill, so I suppose my anxious thoughts were expressing themselves in my face. I told her what had happened the year before. We soon rounded a corner and there I was in exactly the place on the eastern wall where I had felt the urge to jump over the top; only now there was a chain round the stone seat on which I had sat. I did not remember having seen it on my previous visit. I mentioned the chain to Philip who had been reading up on the history of Masada. 'That's easy to explain,' the guide said. 'That's where the women took turns to throw boulders and stones down on the Roman soldiers to stop them climbing up.' Then I realized that the heavy feeling in my hands the year before could have come from holding a big stone. Perhaps in an earlier existence I

189

had indeed hurled myself over the top with such a stone in my hands.

Many of my strangest experiences latterly have occurred overseas. I was on a working visit to Switzerland recently and I made public appearances or gave sittings in accordance with the arrangements made for me by the organizers of my tour. In such circumstances I hardly ever know anything about the people who have appointments to see me, less even than at home when they may write to me or telephone me to make arrangements, in which case I will at least know their names. I prefer to see people individually but I did not demur when I learnt in Switzerland that an appointment had been made for a married couple to see me together.

They came in and within a few minutes their daughter came to me from the spirit world and told me that she had had an accident on the mountains and had died the previous week. She gave her name and a great deal of information that was relevant to her parents, including the fact that she had a sister. The couple confirmed that the dead girl had been buried only two days before they came to see me. The girl then described how she had died. She had been on a training climb at the time but had not been roped because the guide had not thought that the terrain was steep enough or dangerous enough to make this advisable.

She then told me that her sister would shortly be going on the same climb and must be roped, but that her parents, who had booked the climb in the same area in 1983 to see where the accident had taken place, must not go. It was all right for her sister, properly roped, but not for her parents.

When I work, I always have a cross on a table. I regard it as providing both protection and a useful function. I had it in place, as usual, when this Swiss couple came for their sitting. It was not there when they left. I did not for a second think that they had taken it, but where could it be?

190

No one but the man and wife, apart from myself, had been in the room. They spoke English and I did not need an interpreter. Jenny Pestalozzi, with whose parents I was staying, brought me a coffee and we searched everywhere for the cross, but to no avail. It had dematerialized.

Just as suddenly it materialized again, in its correct place on the table. This time however white cotton was twisted all around it. Where the cotton had come from I had no idea because there was no cotton in the room. Jenny rushed into the garden to tell her parents, whose later interpretation of this strange incident coincided with mine: the cotton was symbolic of the rope that the dead girl should have been tied up with, and it was her message to emphasize that her sister should be roped when she made the climb. I can only conclude that the dead girl borrowed the cross for this specific purpose.

A second Swiss happening also provided evidence that in certain circumstances people in the spirit world can cause occurrences in our world. The Pestalozzis and I had been invited to dinner by a woman whose deceased husband had been a lawyer. During his lifetime he had constructed a special fireplace, surrounded by three walls, so that the family could on occasions have a barbecue and eat in the garden by firelight, as on this beautiful summer evening.

Halfway through dinner, my hostess's dead husband started to talk to me. He mentioned a particular name and told me, in English, to repeat it to his wife. I turned to her and said, 'I have your husband here and he's calling this name.' When I gave the name she jumped up and said, 'That's our private name and nobody else knows that!' Whereupon the fire exploded like gunfire, the embers flew into the air and we were soon surrounded by thick black smoke.

When we had all got over our surprise, the lady of the house said, 'That's just the sort of thing my husband would do. He always had to be noticed,' and she told us that she herself had laid the fire that morning, using nothing more than twigs and wood.

I had never been levitated until I went to Finland in 1980, and I had not been so strongly convinced of my own reincarnation until I went to Israel in 1981. I have already described how I saw an object that might have been a flying saucer on the same visit to Switzerland in 1982 to which I have just referred. Although I have been concerned with the 'unknown' for most of my life, it is interesting to me to observe that I am learning more about it every day.

# Chapter Eighteen

So what does it all mean? I regret that I must disappoint any reader who thinks I have all the answers. Very unusual things have been revealed to me and I realized early in life that I had certain gifts, which I have sought to develop. But this is no more than any sensible person will do. One must always make the most of one's advantages and, for that matter, of one's disadvantages. We all have the possibility of progression in this life and it is wrong not to try to develop. A person, for example, who recognizes that he has been born with a gift to play the piano will be very foolish to ignore that gift if by hard work he can bring it to fruition. That is not to say that he is cut out to be a concert pianist, but he will never know unless he makes the effort. This is what I have been impelled to do.

God has given me the gifts of clairvoyance and healing, and I have tried to learn how and why I function, but that has been very difficult, and although I feel that I know a great deal, as I have said I do not know all the answers. Now that I am approaching the twilight of my life, I live in hope that much more is still to be revealed to me. I shall welcome it because we must all develop our gifts and try to become better people.

Like most psychics, I believe that my job is to help other people, and that has always been my motivation, particularly with my healing. I do not put myself in the place of the doctor, the psychiatrist, the priest or the social worker – or of anybody whose function it is to help; but the justification for my work is that I have been able to bring physical and mental comfort to thousands.

So convinced am I about the value of spiritual mediumship that I have spent considerable time in recent years in
teaching this subject. It is not something that anybody can
learn in twelve easy lessons. We need great patience and the
desire to sit for progression. There is always something new
to learn, and I maintain that there are no developed
mediums; we are all developing.

Psychics come in many varied forms, in all shapes and
sizes, and the advice I would give to the millions of people
across the world who seek their help is to use commonsense
about any advice that may be given. Always remember that
a message is invariably tinged with the psychic's personality; it must be so since it comes out of his mental capacity
and has to be interpreted by him in the way he knows best.
If therefore you are told something that offends against your
better judgement, think seriously and then do what you
think to be right. I help and guide everybody but they must
paddle their own canoe. I am not a cushion for people to lie
on.

There has been much talk about so-called fraudulent
mediums. Perhaps they exist, but if so they are no different
from fraudulent accountants or fraudulent salesmen. To be
deliberately dishonest is to act against God's law. We are all
answerable for our gifts and some time, somewhere, we
must account for what we have done with them.

I have referred to the fact that a medium must interpret a
message that he gets from the spirit world. Perhaps I should
elaborate slightly by explaining how a clairvoyant operates.
Clairvoyance, derived from the French for clear seeing, and
clairaudience, similarly derived from clear hearing, are in
practice applied only to vision and hearing in an extension
beyond our normal. Clairvoyance is sometimes called soul
sight.

Scientists are gradually being forced to admit that our
mind field is larger than, and possibly independent of, the

194

brain. This means that all psychic work through normal physical channels is partially or sometimes wholly inoperative. Sensing, seeing and hearing are to me all part of *knowing*. Sometimes I see quite sharply with normal sight; sometimes I see visions, quite clearly; and sometimes I hear a voice, pick up a thought or feel a personality. Results are obtained by different psychics in different ways. We speak of objective clairvoyance, when the spirit personality projects a distinctly physical appearance, and subjective clairvoyance, when the medium discerns from within, from the interior side of his consciousness; and the two often merge. But however a psychic obtains results, he must interpret in his own way what he sees or hears.

Interpretation is as valuable as sight itself because very often those who communicate with us and wish to reach us do so by symbols, which the medium must examine in the light of his knowledge and beliefs, using his intuition. I have often told my students that symbols are a quick way of picking up a message for a sitter. They are a form of shorthand and every psychic must develop his own shorthand so as to be able to interpret his symbols.

Clairvoyance is said to be extended sight but psychics are often puzzled to account for the actual process by which they receive information. A degree of telepathic communication with the sitter cannot always be ruled out and very often a psychic obtains results by a mixture of methods.

I have dealt principally with mental mediumship but I have said very little or nothing about physical mediumship. The latter is a more spectacular means by which those in spirit can manifest themselves, and therefore is more convincing to the sort of people who are looking for physical signs. Some people are unwilling to believe what someone else tells them. Physical mediumship is however a very exhausting business, and it does require a great deal of energy and patience on the part of the medium, because in

195

every case he must go into deep trance. In fact it is not an exaggeration to say that a medium puts his life at risk when he operates thus.

Physical mediums are quite rare and very often die at an early age. I began to sit for physical mediumship myself and I remember what a draining process it was, but because healing was more important to me I chose after some years – although I had quite a good physical circle in operation – to concentrate on healing. When I first began to heal, it was necessary for me to go into trance. Nowadays, I feel there is no advantage in it because I can get results without doing so.

I have seen and experienced physical mediumship in its various forms. Usually the psychic who wishes to demonstrate this gift will sit with a group of people who arrange themselves in a circle, sometimes in a red light, sometimes in the dark. He draws the power from his sitters. After a demonstration of this nature, there is always a very strange, earthy smell in the atmosphere, particularly when ectoplasm has appeared, as it sometimes does, from the medium's body. I have seen it come from the nose or throat or the solar plexus of a psychic.

It comes in waves and may curl on the floor around a sitter's feet, and at the end of the sitting it will return to the medium's body. I have actually touched it, although one must only touch any physically manifested phenomenon if invited to do so, because one may otherwise injure the medium concerned.

Scientists recognize the existence of protoplasm, the basis of life in plants and animals, and there is probably some connection with ectoplasm that comes from the body of the psychic who is demonstrating this particular phenomenon. Protoplasm has been described as transparent or translucent, and ectoplasm is very similar although it varies in density. Sometimes it is like a veil, sometimes like a white mist, and when I touched it, it felt not unlike a cobweb. You can imagine how this manifestation impresses sitters. Exactly what it is I do not know, but I am absolutely certain that it exists.

I have also by invitation touched my dead father and shaken hands with one of my guides. This gave me a strange feeling. I was not frightened. They felt cold, and it was almost like touching plastic.

The especially interesting point about physical mediumship is that everybody in the gathering is able to hear and see the same things. I have seen a spirit build up from the floor in front of my eyes, and voices can be heard around a room or in a particular corner. When I sat to develop this gift, before I decided to concentrate on healing, we used a radiogram to play music, which many psychics believe helps to create a receptive atmosphere; and the music was often speeded up or slowed down by the spirit world during the sittings. Objects have been lifted up from the floor into the air, just the way I was levitated out of bed in Finland. Objects can in fact appear apparently from nowhere. On one occasion a bunch of roses dropped into my lap, and they were wet with dew. We who have this particular knowledge call this phenomenon an apport.

A most interesting apport concerned my father. When he died, I had his body brought home to my house in a coffin – it was my mother's wish – while I made arrangements for the funeral. My mother was living in Leigh-on-Sea at that time and she came to stay with me. As you know, on such occasions friends call in to pay their respects. My father was lying in my lounge with the curtains drawn, as was usual in those days following a death in a house, but I thought how awful it was for him to be left in the dark. So I suggested to my mother – and she agreed – that we should have at least some dim light in the room. I got a pair of steps, climbed up and substituted a 40-watt bulb for the

197

brighter one in the ceiling light. As I was doing so, I heard something drop onto the top of the coffin with a tinkling sound. When I got down again, I looked to see what it was that had fallen. Could it have been something from the light? I found it was a half-crown coin. I was amazed and went to tell my mother. 'Give it to me,' she said, 'I'd like to keep it.' And keep it, I believe, she did to the day of her death.

It was not long after my father's death that I had a very strange experience that made a great impression on me. Indeed, it is just as though it happened yesterday. I was attending a spiritualist service and the psychic who was demonstrating was a very old Cockney medium called Florrie Thompson. I was in the audience and she picked me out for a message. I was not working professionally in those days; my involvement in spiritualism was purely on a social basis with a few friends.

She said, 'I have your father with me and he tells me that you are going to sit with a physical medium.'

A physical medium called William Olsen was shortly to make one of his periodic visits to this church, but because his sittings were very attractive to local spiritualists, entry was by ticket and the twenty or so seats were invariably quickly booked, usually by the important people in the movement, of whom I was certainly not one. All the seats had in fact been reserved for Mr Olsen's next visit, so assuming it was he whom my father had in mind, I said I did not think it was possible for me to sit with a physical medium.

Florrie insisted. 'Oh, yes,' she said, 'I have your father here. He says he wants to talk to you, but he will do so personally through a physical medium, not through me.' She paused for a moment. 'And to prove who he is,' she suddenly went on, 'your father will follow a sister of mercy.'

I thanked the medium for her message but did not lay

much store by it. I was rather sceptical in those days, always doubting, always testing. Three days before the Olsen meeting, however, a woman came to me and said she had two tickets and her friend was unable to use one of them; would I care to buy it? 'I certainly would,' I said quickly, and in this way I became after all the proud possessor of a ticket.

I must explain that William Olsen was what is known as an independent voice medium, and he generally employed what are called trumpets, although they are not in fact trumpets but lightweight cone-shaped objects, through which voices are projected. I had never attended one of his sittings, but I knew his reputation; interesting phenomena were invariably associated with him and strange things were said to occur.

The day came, and of course vividly in my mind was the message I had received that my father would be coming to talk to me. I was hoping that this would be the case, but I did not discuss it with anybody. I went to the meeting and we sat with the medium in a circle. He asked the ladies, whom he thought could sew better than the men, to sew him into his jacket. Using a needle and thread, we stitched him up very strongly from the top of his jacket to the bottom. He then asked the men to tie him in an armchair. They roped his arms to the chair very tightly indeed. We were not sitting in the dark; the hall was illuminated with a red light and we could see him quite clearly all the time. Gradually he went into trance.

I was young and inexperienced, and I marvelled at the wonderful things that happened. The cones flew up and danced in midair and tapped rhythmically on the ceiling, beating time to the singing of the sitters; Mr Olsen liked his audience to sing, no doubt feeling that music created vibrations that he thought were helpful to his work. Then voices were heard from the spirit world with messages for

199

various people in the circle. One of them announced herself as a nun – surely the sister of mercy whom my father had said would precede him – and she spoke not to me but to another of the sitters. I waited expectantly.

Sure enough, no sooner had she finished speaking than the loud voice of my father boomed out right the way round the room. 'I want to talk to my daughter,' he announced. For some reason, perhaps remembering that other people may have heard the message I had been given some time before, I did not rush to respond. The voice persisted. 'I'm George Campbell Cooper, and I want to talk to my daughter, Doris Cooper.'

Nobody there knew that Cooper was my maiden name because by this time I had been Mrs Lawless for several years, and everybody knew me as Doris Lawless, but I still did not answer. I recall that the whole situation seemed to me most unreal. And then one of the trumpets shot down in front of me from wherever it had been and boxed me round the ears and banged me on the head! As it did so, my father's voice ordered me to reply. 'Speak up, speak up, Doris, I'm your father.'

You may imagine how shocked I was. 'Hello, Dad, hello, Dad,' I managed to stammer, 'I'm sorry.' We then conversed for a little while until my father amazed me by saying, 'I have your son with me. He has come to speak to you.'

I have already said that I lost a son who had lived for only sixteen hours. I am positive that nobody in that gathering knew about this. The baby had been christened John and had been buried while I was still in hospital. And now I felt him climb on my lap and put his arms round my neck. I was so overcome that I cannot say I actually saw him, although the women sitting on either side of me did so. I felt him and heard him say, 'Hello, Mummy.'

Can you grasp what this would do to a mother? I was

absolutely flabbergasted. It was so impressive. I really do not know much about what else went on during the sitting because all I could think of was my son and my father.

I do remember how the proceedings ended. A voice told us that our medium would be levitated and put in the centre of our circle, and that we should not be worried about it. Suddenly there was a bang and Mr Olsen was lifted up in his chair. When the red light was turned off and the main lights switched on, he was sitting in the armchair in the middle of the circle, unroped and without his jacket. The ropes were on the floor. His jacket was in a corner of the room, still completely sewn up with not a stitch undone.

What a wonderful experience that was for me! My father had spoken to me, and my son had come to greet me. Of course magicians can do seemingly miraculous things, but William Olsen was no magician. He was a strange little man who would have had to be more than a magician to have performed all he did in a red light in front of a group of experienced people. I did sit with him again but I was never lucky enough to get a message such as I did at the first time of sitting. He died at quite an early age about three years after my first impressive encounter with him.

In one sense there is no such thing as death because even the physical body takes up another form when we pass over. It is not the physical part of us that survives however in the spirit world. It is that indefinable entity – the immaterial part of us that we call the soul – that continues to exist. The body is merely the envelope that houses the soul within each one of us. The soul, although the centre of ourselves, is not shut up in the material body like a bird in a cage; it can manifest itself outside the body as light or sound; and when I contact someone from the spirit world, it is the memory bank or link with the mind and soul which communicates with me. In other words, the spirit person who wants to communicate produces a picture of himself as he wants to be seen by me.

201

It is very difficult to write about this subject in simple terms, and this is not an easy concept. The word 'soul' is used in many different ways. Sometimes it is used to designate the principle of life, in which sense, figuratively speaking, I would describe it as an animated spark that has emanated from the life force – God, in whom I believe – and I think that we must at some time have broken away from this great source of energy and that when it becomes possible for us to be perfected, we shall be embraced back. Until such time – and remember that we are talking about infinity, time without beginning or end – we must pass through many stages of existence. We may make very little progress in one existence and a great deal in another.

I not only believe in life after death; I believe also in reincarnation. The feeling that one has lived before is common to many people, and I incline to the opinion of Allan Kardec, the name under which a nineteenth-century French investigator of reincarnation wrote a number of books on the subject, based upon personal evidence, some of it gathered as a result of sitting with mediums. Kardec believed that the next world is a very busy place, not unlike this world, and peopled with spirits leading useful lives and undergoing a period of preparation in which the soul consciously readies itself for higher development.

Some people believe that when spirits desire to return to earth for further development, they may be able sometimes to select the family into which they are born. This idea may seem very strange until we realize that, being free from matter when we become part of the spirit world, we then judge things differently from the way we do now. Perhaps then we make a particular decision why we must return to earth and why we must go through the trial of living in human form; and perhaps then we know the purpose of this trial and that we are returning for progression rather than simply for the enjoyments of earth. Perhaps after each existence on earth we can assess what we have accomplished and what we still need to achieve.

Based upon much evidence I have received, I know that some of us do not progress very far on the road to perfection. There are evil people and people who are born into an environment that is not conducive to easy progression. Heaven and hell are not places but states of being. Heaven is nearness to God, hell is remoteness from God. These states exist in this life as well as in the life beyond. I believe that there are many stages in the spirit world, many spheres of existence, and that we pass to the state of existence of which we have knowledge. As Jesus said, 'In my Father's house are many mansions.'

Anyone familiar with the New Testament will know that in the third chapter of St John, Jesus said to Nicodemus: 'Except a man be born again, he cannot see the kingdom of God.' And when Nicodemus asked, 'How can a man be born when he is old? Can he enter the second time into his mother's womb, and be born?', Jesus replied: 'Except a man be born of water and of the Spirit, he cannot enter the kingdom of God. That which is born of the flesh is flesh and that which is born of the Spirit is spirit. Marvel not that I say unto thee, Ye must be born again.'

The soul, being a spiritual and not a physical entity, is not destroyed when the human body dies. It is connected with the body during life on earth but continues to shine and exist when the body is no more. If you look at your face in the mirror, your face will still be there if you remove the mirror, although you can no longer see its reflection. It is the same with the soul.

Each soul comes into existence during birth and is a unique creation, and physical existence on earth is a necessary experience for the soul. Life is a stage of existence when a human being has a chance to develop spiritual qualities, such as love, compassion, generosity and truthfulness, all of which we need after our physical existence ceases. We have an opportunity to develop these qualities on earth in the same way that a child develops in its mother's womb. A child in the womb cannot use all its faculties but its future existence would be very limited without them.

About the reality of reincarnation I am in no doubt. I know that when we die, someone comes to meet us. We are never left without a guiding hand. The death of the body is not something to be feared, but welcomed as a birth to a fuller life.

# Chapter Nineteen

I believe that we come to this life for a specific purpose. There is a time to be born and a time to die, and some of us do not need to live many years on this earth plane. Some of us are here however not only for our own progression but to help others, the people whose lives we touch. I was once asked to visit a little girl in Dagenham. She had fallen while on roller-skates and had developed a tumour. I went every week for seven months although I had the feeling within me that I might not be able to help her physically; but I knew that nothing would be lost because I would certainly be able to help her spiritually.

The child looked forward to my visits but I sensed a deep unhappiness between her parents, probably because of their daughter's illness. Eventually she died, and after her death they came to see me and asked me whether I had known that they had been planning to divorce but that when their little girl had become ill, this had drawn them very close together. Because of my visits and the consequent improvement in the child's attitude towards her own condition – her personality, they said, had changed and she had become a lot happier – they realized that healing was important, and they asked whether they could learn to become healers. They worked together and their lives changed completely.

So who is to say that this little girl's short life on this earth was not just for the purpose of making her parents see things differently?

Incidentally, I believe that when a child is born very afflicted, he must be a very old spiritual soul who has assumed more than his natural burden in order to help a weaker soul. This is what some eastern religions call the law of karma – the law of cause and effect. Do we know why many things happen in our lives – perhaps, we feel sometimes, by accident? Is there not maybe a pattern in this 'accident' that changes the whole of our lives and affects other people's lives too?

A very curious incident occurred to me just after the end of the Falklands conflict in 1982. A lady telephoned me on behalf of a friend. 'Is your name Doris Collins?' she asked, and when I said yes, 'Are you Doris Collins the clairvoyant?' she enquired. When she was satisfied that I was indeed the person she was seeking, she asked whether I could see a friend of hers who needed me most urgently. My business appointments diary was very full and I was unable to arrange a very early meeting, but following a last-minute cancellation I was able after all to fit the caller's friend in the next day.

I telephoned the caller who said would I mind if she accompanied her friend, who was very nervous. They arrived together and sat with me, and we had quite wonderful results. The lady who wanted to see me was a Mrs Gillon. I asked her no questions. As we sat, both her parents came to me, and her father described exactly many aspects of his life. Most strangely, he kept offering me a needle and thread, and I saw him sewing, as if working on a tapestry, which was quite unusual for a man. Mrs Gillon told me that her father had been wounded in the 1914-18 war and the nurses had taught him what later became his hobby. He made and sold a great many tapestries.

Then a young man came who was rather chatty with me, and quite a humorist. 'My name's John,' he said, 'and I'm not a bird.' I was not sure what he meant and whether it was worth relaying his message; but when he repeated it, I passed it on. Mrs Gillon said, 'I understand.' John then said, 'I've got to talk to Florrie,' and apparently Mrs

Gillon's Christian name was Florence, although I did not know that. John enquired why his friend Barry's motorbike was in another friend's garden. That might sound a very trivial question to anybody listening but it quite stunned Mrs Gillon because her son Barry had actually taken the bike to a friend's garden to be repaired.

The young man, who had insisted that he was not a bird, then said 'I am flying now. I have got my wings.' And he used words that I cannot ever forget: 'They got me,' he said, 'on the last knockings.' He also told me that he had lain for a long time in a very cold place until he had been picked up.

I did not know exactly what all this meant, but it clearly meant a great deal to Mrs Gillon, and the strangest thing about this story is what she later told me. She said that she had had a dream that had made such an impression on her that she had told a friend about it – the friend who contacted me. According to Mrs Gillon, she dreamt that she was in a hall with a lot of people. There was a woman sitting on a platform who got up and said, 'Good evening, ladies and gentlemen, my name is Doris Collins and I have a message here from a boy who was killed in the Falklands who says his name is John and he wants to talk to a lady called Mrs G.' Mrs Gillon immediately rose and said, 'I'm Mrs G. People call me Mrs G. It's how I sign my letters.' The lady on the platform, who had identified herself as Doris Collins, summoned Mrs Gillon to the front of the hall and asked her to kneel. She then gave her John's message that he was lying on a cliff and was very cold but would be returning.

So much for the dream. Mrs Gillon knew nothing at all about psychic visions and she had never heard of me. She did however know a young man named John Crow who had joined the Third Parachute Regiment and had sailed to the Falklands on the *Canberra*. I believe he was a friend

207

of Mrs Gillon's son and stayed with the family when he was in the district; Mrs Gillon regarded herself as a sort of second mother to him.

The tragic fact is that John Crow was killed forty-eight hours before the Argentinians surrendered and two days before Mrs Gillon's amazing dream in which she was given my name. Following the dream, she woke up in a terrible sweat and could not get back to sleep. She told her friend who said, 'What a strange thing! I wonder if there is a Doris Collins.' Mrs Gillon happens to live in Ham, not far from where I live in Richmond, and her friend got out the local telephone directory and found my name, which is how she came to ring me.

When later she heard about the young man's death, the words he spoke to her in her dream and the words he spoke to her through me all made sense. His surname perhaps explains his facetious reference to not being a bird; and as to his reference to flying and having his wings, Mrs Gillon told me that it had been his ambition to join the air corps and learn to fly. He had also told Mrs Gillon in her dream that he would be returning, and it is interesting that his parents later decided to ask for his body to be brought back for burial in England instead of in the Falklands.

This is a very strange story indeed. Whether the young man had heard about me in his lifetime, I cannot say; but somehow he caused Mrs Gillon to dream about him and to start the chain of events that led her to me, so that I could pass on his messages to her and, through her, to his friends.

I do not believe in coincidence. Everything fits into a plan. But I think that we have the opportunity to decide how to deal with certain problems that are ordained. On the path of life we come to certain milestones, but only to the extent that the milestones exist is our destiny fixed. We can choose how we pass them, and although we are all products of what we have been, progression, as I keep saying, is always open to us.

I believe that our previous incarnations must have a bearing on our present existence. I once had an Oriental gentleman come to see me who was a musician. He came to me because he was beginning to lose the sensation in his right hand when he played the piano, and his hand had started to shake when he was writing. This was a very serious matter to someone who earned his living with his hands. During the sitting with me I picked up many things about his lifestyle. I knew he had a wife and children as well as three mistresses in different parts of the world. I also knew he was drinking far too much, and I told him all these things which he said were quite correct.

As I was talking to him, I saw something come and chop off his right hand. I knew instantly that this had happened to him in a previous incarnation and that it was not something that was going to happen. I told him what I had seen, and he had so vivid a memory flashback that he actually felt the pain. I told him many other things about his life and he agreed with my analysis, saying that he regarded this episode as a pointer in the right direction. So it may indeed have been, but to me it was evidence that he had lived on this earth previously.

The world of spirit has always been part of my life. What seems very strange to some people to me is quite natural. When you grow up in the way that I have, you never think that you will have to explain what is natural to you, any more than you will have to explain how you walk.

The spirit world is around us at all times, but vibrating on a different scale. By raising my rate of vibration and letting the inner sense reach out, I am able to contact those who vibrate on that scale. Sometimes results are better than at other times.

To me life would not be normal without an awareness of the spirit world, but I do not think that this makes me abnormal. Lots of people have great sensing; they *feel* things about people and situations. In my case I have simply learnt the importance of being pliable.

I am not a fortune-teller although a message about the future will often come to me. But people who seek me out expecting me to tell their futures have certainly come to the wrong person. I get feelings about things that are going to happen and occasionally I am able to put them to advantage. For example, my husband Philip and I owned a car with which we were very happy. It was two years old, had been regularly serviced and had given us no problems; and yet gradually I got the feeling that we ought to sell it and buy another.

My husband saw no logical reason to do so, but the feeling kept niggling at me. One day when we were passing a car showroom, I persuaded him to stop and look. He agreed on the understanding that under no circumstances would we buy another car, but when he saw that I was very interested in a particular model, he relented. We talked to the salesman and eventually decided to trade in our existing vehicle, which was taken in for examination and carefully inspected; and because it was apparently in such good condition and had a low mileage, we were given about £200 over the normal figure in exchange.

The new car needed a small adjustment, so a week later I returned to the showroom and saw the salesman who had attended to us. In conversation he asked me whether I had ever had any trouble putting the old car into reverse. 'Good gracious, no,' I said, 'why do you ask?' He told me that he had personally used the car for four or five days, and then one morning he found that he could not reverse it. He had taken it to the workshop where it was discovered that it needed a whole new gear-box at a cost of about £200. I felt terribly guilty and, bearing in mind that this was the amount we had been paid over the odds, I offered to pay for the repair. He would not hear of it. 'No,' he said, 'we are a big company and a deal is a deal.' They had in any case inspected the car very carefully before agreeing terms.

'I had a feeling that I ought to change the car,' I said apologetically.

I had to chuckle at the salesman's reply. 'Madam,' he said, 'you must be psychic.'

That is a very minor instance where my gift was used to my personal advantage. I remember one occasion during my early years as a healer when a patient asked me casually which horse was going to win the Derby. I hardly ever gamble or have a bet and I just answered him very quickly with the first thought that came into my head: 'Lester Piggott's mount.' 'Oh,' he said, surprised, 'he's never ridden a Derby winner.' Piggott at the time was a very young man and I am not sure how I even knew his name. I knew nothing about horseracing and had never seen a horserace. Unknown to me, my patient backed the horse and told his friends. When the race was over, he came and told me that he had won quite a considerable amount of money by backing the horse on which Lester Piggott won his first Derby.

I would never use my gifts for that sort of purpose. I am in any case too busy with my work to be interested in gambling. I have only played roulette twice. The first occasion was when I went to Monte Carlo. It was the thing to do there. I could not stop winning; I seemed to know just where to place my chips. People crowded around me excitedly, but when I began to feel an urge taking control of me, I decided that that was the moment to stop. I tried my luck once again in a casino on a ship. This time I broke even, perhaps because I did not want to bring my mind to bear on the possibility of predicting winning numbers.

I do not believe in taking advantage of my gifts for trivial purposes. To do so would devalue them. But we must always be ready to accept help that is offered to us from whatever source. An admirable example of such help was given to me by my friend Marjorie Horton, who accompanied me to the Philippines. It made such an impression on her that she says it changed her whole life, causing her to take an interest in the psychic and become a very proficient healer. She was theatre sister at the time in a very big hospital when a little boy was brought in with a tumour of the brain. A most experienced surgeon operated but the child died a few days later. Almost exactly a year afterwards, his young sister was brought into the same hospital with a similar tumour of the brain.

The nurses were very disturbed, for they remembered the previous occasion and thought how terrible it would be if both the children suffered the same fate. The same surgeon operated on the little girl, as he had done before on her brother, and skilful as he was, he was very unsure about whether he would be able to save the second child.

He went home after the operation and told his wife how worried he was. She took an interest in psychic matters and knew the value of prayer; so, at her suggestion, they sat together in meditation, asking for help and guidance to save the child. As they were sitting there, the surgeon had a mental vision. He saw the old professor who had taught him surgery, who told him: 'The child can be saved if you follow my directions.'

'I don't know what else to do,' the surgeon said. 'I've done all I can.'

'I will guide your hand,' came the reply, 'but you must operate again.'

The surgeon immediately telephoned an exhausted Marjorie Horton and summoned her to return to the hospital and prepare the theatre for another operation when the child came round. She thought he must be drunk and asked what had happened. 'I can't discuss it with you now,' he said, 'just do as I tell you.'

She went back, did all that was necessary and awaited the surgeon's arrival. The child was later brought back to the theatre, the surgeon came in, scrubbed up and started to operate. Marjorie says that there was a strange feeling in the room, and not a word was spoken; it seemed unnecessary. The surgeon's hand seemed somehow to be guided. She did not of course know at the time what had happened when the surgeon had gone home.

After the operation, he told her about his vision. He also said that he felt that his old teacher's hand had been over his, guiding him to do something different from what he had done before.

The child recovered.

To me this is a supreme example of love at work. The surgeon operated with love, but a love made more powerful by help from the spirit world. As far as healing is concerned, love to me is the most important element. If a baby falls, its mother will immediately pick it up tenderly and nurse it. The very act of touching seems to make it better. That is simply natural healing, springing from natural love, and that is the principle on which healers operate.

'Doris is different,' my mother said. I know what she meant, but in truth we are all different although we have much in common. We are all individuals. But even if there are degrees of difference and I am more different than most, I think I remain an ordinary woman.

# Epilogue

In this short book I have been able to describe only a few of the experiences of my varied life. I should like to have written an instructional book, and perhaps one day I shall, dealing with the various matters concerning development. For many years I held classes in this subject and many of my students are now on the public platform, but I have been unable to hold such classes recently owing to my travelling.

The purpose of the book would be to help the youth of today who are interested in all the spiritual paths, realizing as so many of us do that without a return to real values, there is little hope for the world. Love and fellowship can conquer all, with God's help, and strife and suffering are the result of the materialistic outlook so prevalent today.

To develop psychic powers by whatever means is highly dangerous unless one acknowledges the Supreme Power, the source of all life. The searcher after truth and revelation must be prompted by the highest motives. Of course we mortals do not always achieve this ideal but when developing, it is essential to have the will to serve humanity. Development for selfish reasons cannot have beneficial results in the long run.

So much on all fronts, both religious and secular, is of no benefit to mankind, and in many cases is actually injurious. Love and unity are what we must aim for, hatred and discord what we must cast aside. Malice and greed are rife in the world. If a person wishes to develop in order to have power over his fellow men or to obtain the recognition that comes from riches, he is doomed to ultimate failure, as it is against the laws of nature. Humility and honesty must be the guide. Without these you are wasting your time.

When consulting a psychic medium, a guru or a teacher of any sort, there is little point in having preconceived notions of the outcome. I have already said that in my opinion there are no developed persons on earth, although many are further along the path than others.

The truth can only be revealed to those of us who are able to clear our minds of worldly matters. That is the purpose of meditation. Worry and unhappiness are its twin enemies, but that is not to say that suffering can or should be avoided. Indeed, physical suffering may be an essential part of the karmic path.

At the front of this book I thanked many of the dear ones who are so close to me on this earth plane. May I now thank the many others in different spheres of existence who have also helped in the most difficult periods of my life? And to all of you, dear readers, may God add blessing and give you the realization that life lived here to its fullest extent is of the greatest importance to our individual progression.